BASIC
SPANISH

Juan Kattán-Ibarra was born in Chile, and has travelled extensively in Spain and Latin America. He has degrees from the University of Chile, Michigan State University, Manchester University and the Institute of Education, London University. He has taught Spanish at Ealing College and Shell International and has been an examiner in Spanish for the London Chamber of Commerce and Industry and the University of London School Examinations Board. He is the author of *Teach Yourself Spanish*, *ECO: A Spanish Practice Book*, *Basic Spanish Conversation*, and co-author of *Spain after Franco*, *Working with Spanish*, *Mundo Nuevo* and *Se Escribe Así*.

TEACH YOURSELF BOOKS

BASIC SPANISH

Juan Kattán-Ibarra

TEACH YOURSELF BOOKS
Hodder and Stoughton

First published 1988
Second impression 1989

Copyright © 1988
Juan Kattán-Ibarra

British Library Cataloguing in Publication Data

Kattán-Ibarra, Juan
  Basic Spanish.—(Teach yourself books).
  1. Spanish language—For non-Spanish
  speaking students
  I. Title
  468.2′4

ISBN 0 340 420782

Printed and bound in Great Britain
for Hodder and Stoughton Educational,
a division of Hodder and Stoughton Ltd,
Mill Road, Dunton Green, Sevenoaks, Kent
by
Richard Clay Ltd Bungay Suffolk

Typeset by Macmillan India Ltd., Bangalore 560025.

Contents

Introduction

This course is intended for those who are starting Spanish. It will also serve those who wish to revise the main structures of the language following a grammatically oriented approach. The book may be used independently or in conjunction with another coursebook. The emphasis is on grammar usage and the vocabulary has been chosen to cover the essential communicative needs of the student. Approximately 1100 words have been used, all taken from Un Nivel Umbral (a threshold level) of the Council of Europe. Explanations are simple and have been illustrated by means of carefully selected sentences and dialogues which place the language within a useful context. All this, together with the language practice provided, should enable the student to acquire a knowledge of all the essential structures of Spanish and to use the language accurately in everyday situations.

The book consists of 37 graded units, each one covering one or two language points. In most cases the title of the unit indicates the language which is being studied: Describing (Unit 5), Expressing possession (Unit 7), Making comparisons (Unit 9). Other titles express the contents in grammatical terms: Nouns, adjectives and adverbs (Unit 2), Passive and impersonal expressions (Unit 17). Grammar coverage is extensive. It includes the study of grammatical concepts such as nouns, adjectives, adverbs, pronouns and prepositions as well as the whole range of simple and compound tenses, including the subjunctive. Particular emphasis has been placed on the study of certain verbs which may pose a problem to English speakers, e.g. *ser* and *estar* (to be).

Most units follow a similar pattern, beginning with brief explanations of the language in question with occasional references to English to illustrate the difference between the two languages. The forms, e.g. verb tables, adjectives, pronouns, are then clearly laid out and are followed by illustrative sentences and dialogues which set the structures within a communicative context. To consolidate all this the

Practique sections (Practice) present exercises. Some of these are grammatical, others are of a communicative nature. The key to these exercises will be found at the back of the book, followed by two appendices, which include such information as a list of numbers and verb tables, and then a useful vocabulary.

How to use this book

The following procedure is suggested for working through each unit: read the notes in English which explain the grammatical point or language function which is being analysed. Then go on to the new forms and illustrative sentences and study these with reference to the preceding explanation. The English translation should help you to understand fully the meaning of each sentence. Once you have had enough experience with the language you may find it useful to make up other similar sentences to reinforce your knowledge of the new forms and structures. If the section includes a dialogue (*Diálogo*), read this and see how the new language functions within a longer context. Most of the vocabulary used in the dialogue will be known to you from previous units. New words will appear with their English translation next to the dialogue. If you have difficulty remembering the meaning of certain words you may refer to the Spanish–English vocabulary at the end of the book. The dialogues deal with everyday situations and have been kept brief to help you learn them. In order to assimilate the new language you may find it useful to read the dialogue several times and try to repeat it without looking at the book.

You may now proceed with the Practice (*Practique*) which generally follows the dialogue. Each exercise is preceded by an instruction in English. By now you should be able to do these exercises without reference to the explanatory notes. If you find difficulty with a particular exercise, it may be convenient to revise the whole section or unit. If necessary, check your answers in the Key.

Longer units have been divided into sections and you may study each section in the way outlined above until you have completed the whole unit. Because of their nature, Units 1, 2, 36 and 37 do not contain exercises or dialogues but only explanatory notes and examples.

1 Pronunciation guide

The aim of this brief pronunciation guide is to offer hints which will enable you to produce sounds recognizable to a speaker from any part of the Spanish-speaking world. It cannot by itself teach you to pronounce Spanish accurately. The best way to acquire a reasonably good accent is to listen and try to imitate native speakers.

Listed below are the main elements of Spanish pronunciation and their approximate English equivalents.

1 Vowels

Spanish vowels are generally shorter, clearer and more precise than English vowels. Unstressed vowels are not weakened as in English but are given much the same value in pronunciation as those which are stressed. For example, in the English word *comfortable*, the vowels which follow the syllable *com* are weak, while in Spanish every vowel in the word *confortable* has the same quality.

There are only five vowel sounds in Spanish:

a	like the *u* in *butter, cut*	casa	costa
e	like the *e* in *belt, end*	él	ejemplo
i	like the *i* in *marine*, or the *ea* in *mean*	mirar	Isabel
o	like the *o* in *model, god*	sol	hola
u	like the *u* in *rude* or the *oo* in *moon*	uno	mucho

Note:

When **i** occurs before another vowel, it is pronounced like the *y* in *yes*.	tiene	prefiere
When **u** occurs before another vowel, it is pronounced like the *w* in *wind*.	aduana	bueno
After **q**, **u** is not pronounced at all.	quien	que
u is also silent in **gui** and **gue**.	guía	pague

u is pronounced in **güi** and **güe**,
a very infrequent sound combination
in Spanish.

lingüística
vergüenza

2 Consonants

The pronunciation of Spanish consonants is generally similar to that
of English consonants. But note the following features:

b and **v**	in initial position and after **n** are pronounced the same, like the *b* in *bar*	**B**arcelona	in**v**itación
	in other positions more like the *v* in *very*	Se**v**illa	tra**b**ajo
c	before **a, o, u** like the *c* in *coast*	**c**osta	**c**astellano
c	before **e, i** like the *th* in *thin*	**c**ero	gra**c**ias
ch	like the *ch* in *chair*	**Ch**ile	dere**ch**a
d	like the *d* in *day*	**d**ía	an**d**ar
	between vowels and after **r**, like the *th* in *those*	na**d**a	Cór**d**oba
g	before **a, o, u** like the *g* in *government*	**g**ordo	la**g**o
	before **e, i** like a strong *h*, or like the Scottish *ch* in *loch*	**g**eneral	**G**ibraltar
j	like a strong *h*, or like the Scottish *ch* in *loch*	**J**orge	naran**j**a
h	is silent	**h**ola	a**h**ora
ll	like the *lli* in *million*	mi**ll**ón	**ll**amar
ñ	like the *ni* in *onion*	ma**ñ**ana	se**ñ**or
q(u)	like the *c* in *cake*	**qu**ien	**qu**e
r	in initial position is strongly rolled	**r**ío	**r**egión
rr	strongly rolled	co**rr**eos	Ta**rr**agona
y	like the *y* in *yes*	ho**y**	ma**y**o
z	like the *th* in *think*	**Z**aragoza	pla**z**a

3 Stress and accentuation

Words which end in a vowel, **n** or **s**
stress the last syllable but one.

nada
toman

ameri**ca**no
chicos

Words which end in a consonant other than **n** or **s** stress the last syllable.	ho**tel** es**pañol** **Madrid** ciu**dad** fe**liz** me**jor**
Words which do not follow the above rules carry a written accent over the stressed syllable.	a**llí** in**glés** auto**bús** invita**ción** te**lé**fono ki**ló**metro
Differences in meaning between certain similar words are shown through the use of an accent.	sí (*yes*) si (*if*) él (*he*) el (*the, masc.*) sé (*I know*) se (*reflexive pronoun*)
Question words carry an accent, and are preceded by an inverted question mark.	¿dónde? (*where?*) ¿cuándo? (*when?*) ¿qué? (*what?*)
Qué carries an accent in exclamations, which are preceded by an inverted exclamation mark.	¡qué lástima! (*what a pity!*) ¡qué interesante! (*how interesting!*)

4 Spelling

Note the following changes in spelling:
Verbs may change their spelling in certain forms in order to keep the sound of the infinitive. For example:

llegar (*to arrive*)	but	lle**gué** (*I arrived*)
coger (*to catch*)	but	co**jo** (*I catch*)
tocar (*to play*)	but	to**qué** (*I played*)

Words which finish in **z** change the **z** into **c** to form the plural:

feliz	feli**ces** (*happy*)
lápiz	lápi**ces** (*pencil/pencils*)

5 Capitalization

Capitalization in Spanish is less extensive than in English. Words which denote nationality, religion, languages, and the names of the months of the year and the days of the week are normally not capitalized.

un inglés	*an Englishman*
un americano	*an American*
un protestante	*a Protestant*
un católico	*a Catholic*
el inglés	*English*
el español	*Spanish*
lunes, martes . . .	*Monday, Tuesday . . .*
enero, febrero . . .	*January, February . . .*

Titles such as **señor, señora, señorita** are not capitalized unless they are abbreviated.

el señor García	*Mr García*
la señora Ramírez	*Mrs Ramírez*
la señorita Ahumada	*Miss Ahumada*

But notice:

el Sr García, la Sra Ramírez, la Srta Ahumada.
Capital letters do not normally carry a written accent.

6   Liaison

If a word ends in a vowel and is followed by a word beginning with a vowel, the two vowels are normally pronounced as though both formed part of the same word. When the two vowels are the same, these are usually pronounced as one. For example:

¿Cómo_está_usted?	*How are you?*
Ella no_está_aquí.	*She's not here.*
¿Habla_español?	*Do you speak Spanish?*

2 Nouns, adjectives and adverbs

Nouns

1 The

All nouns in Spanish are either masculine or feminine and, as in English, they can be singular or plural. The word for *the* is **el** for singular masculine nouns and **la** for singular feminine nouns.

masculine		*feminine*	
el señor	*the gentleman*	**la** señora	*the lady*
el chico	*the boy*	**la** chica	*the girl*

There are only two contractions in the Spanish language. **A** and **el** become **al**, and **de** and **el** become **del**.

al señor   *to the gentleman*
del señor   *of the gentleman*

In the plural **el** becomes **los** and **la** becomes **las**.

los señores	*the gentlemen*	**las** señoras	*the ladies*
los chicos	*the boys*	**las** chicas	*the girls*

2 A / an

The word for *a* is **un** for masculine nouns and **una** for feminine nouns.

masculine		*feminine*	
un amigo	*a boyfriend*	**una** amiga	*a girlfriend*
un hijo	*a son*	**una** hija	*a daughter*

The plural forms **unos, unas** are translated into English as *some*.

unos amigos   *some friends*   **unas** amigas   *some girlfriends*

Spanish does not use the equivalent of English *a* when you indicate your occupation. Compare these two phrases:

>un profesor   *a teacher*
>Soy profesor   *I am a teacher*

3 Masculine or feminine?

Nouns ending in **-o** are usually masculine while nouns ending in **-a** are usually feminine.

masculine	*feminine*
el apartament**o** *the apartment*	la cas**a** *the house*
el bañ**o** *the bathroom*	la cocin**a** *the kitchen*

But as in every rule there are exceptions:

masculine	*feminine*
el programa *the programme*	la radio *the radio*
el día *the day*	la mano *the hand*

To differentiate male from female some nouns change the **-o** to **-a**:

>el amig**o**   *the boyfriend*   la amig**a**   *the girlfriend*

Other nouns which end in a consonant in the masculine have an extra **-a** in the feminine:

>el señor   *the gentleman*   la señor**a**   *the lady*

Many nouns ending in **-e, -l, -n** (not **-ión**), **-r, -s** are masculine:

>el jefe (*the boss*), el animal (*the animal*), el tren (*the train*), el sur (*the south*), el país (*the country*).

Nouns ending in **-ad** and **-ión** are usually feminine:

>la ciudad (*the city*), la estación (*the station*).

Nouns ending in **-ista** can be either masculine or feminine, according to the sex of the person:

>el turista   *the tourist* (*male*)   la turista   *the tourist* (*fem.*)
>el dentista   *the dentist* (*male*)   la dentista   *the dentist* (*fem.*)

Some nouns which denote sex have different masculine and feminine forms:

el padre	*the father*	la madre	*the mother*
el hombre	*the man*	la mujer	*the woman* (also *wife*)

The masculine plural of some nouns may be used to refer to members of both sexes.

los padres   *parents*
los amigos   *friends*

4 Singular and plural

Nouns which end in a vowel form the plural by adding -s:

la señorita	*the young lady*	las señoritas	*the young ladies*
el hombre	*the man*	los hombres	*the men*

Nouns which end in a consonant add **-es**:

el señor	*the gentleman*	los señor**es**	*the gentlemen*
la ciudad	*the city*	las ciudad**es**	*the cities*

Nouns which end in **-z** change the **-z** to **-c** and add **-es**:

el lápiz	*the pencil*	los lápi**ces**	*the pencils*
una vez	*once*	dos ve**ces**	*twice*

Some nouns lose their accent in the plural:

la estación	*the station*	las estaciones	*the stations*
un inglés	*an Englishman*	unos ingleses	*some English people*

Some nouns gain an accent in the plural:

el joven	*the young man*	los jóvenes	*the young men*

Adjectives

1 Agreement of adjectives

Adjectives must show agreement of gender (masculine or feminine) and number (singular or plural) with the noun they describe.

un señor inglés   *an English gentleman*
una señora inglesa   *an English lady*

If the masculine form of the adjective ends in **-o**, the feminine form ends in **-a**.

un amigo americano   *an American friend* (*male*)
una amiga americana   *an American friend* (*female*)

If an adjective ends in a letter other than **-o** or **-a** the feminine form is the same as the masculine.

un país interesante   *an interesting country*
una ciudad interesante   *an interesting city*

To form the plural of adjectives follow the rule as for nouns (see 4 above).

Feminine nouns of nationality or origin end in **-a** (*sing.*) and **-as** (*plural*), even when the masculine noun ends in a consonant.

un chico irlandés   *an Irish boy*
una chica irlandesa   *an Irish girl*

unos chicos irlandeses   *some Irish boys*
unas chicas irlandesas   *some Irish girls*

2   Position of adjectives

Adjectives normally come after the noun they describe.

un amigo escocés   *a Scottish friend*
una mujer interesante   *an interesting woman*

Some adjectives, numbers for instance, come before the noun.

la primera estación   *the first station*
cuatro estaciones   *four stations*

Descriptive adjectives are sometimes placed before the noun to show emphasis, affection or some other desired effect.

un buen restaurante   *a good restaurant*
una pequeña casa   *a little house*

3 Short forms

A few adjectives drop the ending -o when they come before a masculine noun.

primero	*first*	primer piso	*first floor*
tercero	*third*	tercer piso	*third floor*
bueno	*good*	un buen chico	*a good boy*
uno	*one*	un dólar	*one dollar (*or *a dollar)*

Other adjectives which follow the same pattern are:

malo:	mal	*bad*
ninguno:	ningún	*none, no*
alguno:	algún	*some, any*

The adjective **grande** (*large, big*) shortens to **gran** before a masculine or feminine singular noun. When it precedes the noun it usually translates into English as *great*.

un hombre grande
  a big man
un gran hombre
  a great man

una ciudad grande
  a big city
una gran ciudad
  a big (or *great*) *city*

Adverbs

Formation

In English we often form adverbs by adding *-ly* to an adjective, as in *rapidly, slowly*. In Spanish many adverbs are formed by adding **-mente** to the feminine form of the adjective.

rápida	*rapid*	rápidamente	*rapidly*
lenta	*slow*	lentamente	*slowly*

Notice that if the adjective carries an accent, the accent is kept in the adverb.

If the adjective ends in a consonant, simply add **-mente**.

fácil	*easy*	fácilmente	*easily*
difícil	*difficult*	difícilmente	*hardly*

12 *Nouns, adjectives and adverbs*

There are many adverbs which do not end in **-mente**. Here are some examples:

Time:	hoy (*today*), mañana (*tomorrow*)
Place:	aquí (*here*), allí (*there*)
Manner:	bien (*well*), mal (*badly*)
Quantity:	mucho (*a lot*), poco (*little*)

3 I am . . ., you are . . .

1 Subject pronouns

The Spanish equivalent of words such as *I, you, he, she* are as follows:

yo	*I*	**nosotros**/**as**	*we*
tú	*you* (sing., familiar)	**vosotros**/**as**	*you* (pl., fam.)
usted	*you* (sing., formal)	**ustedes**	*you* (pl., formal)
él	*he*	**ellos**	*they* (masc.)
ella	*she*	**ellas**	*they* (fem.)

Notice the feminine plural forms **nosotras, vosotras, ellas**.

Note also that there are two ways of saying *you* in Spanish, a polite form, **usted** (abbreviated **Vd.**), and a friendly or familiar form, **tú**. If one is addressing more than one person these words become **ustedes** (abbreviated as **Vdes.**) and **vosotros** respectively. Generally, you may use the polite form in formal situations, when you don't know someone at all or not very well, or as a sign of respect to older people, for example. Use the friendly form to people you know quite well, of your own age or status, with whom you are on first name terms. However, it must be pointed out that the line between **usted** and **tú** is sometimes difficult to draw. Moreover, the familiar form is becoming more and more common in everyday usage in Spain, even in official situations. Notice that **usted** takes the third person singular (**él, ella**) and that **ustedes** takes the third person plural (**ellos, ellas**) form of the verb.

Subject pronouns are usually omitted in Spanish, except for emphasis or to avoid ambiguity. The form of the verb or its ending is normally sufficient to indicate the subject of the verb.

2 *Ser, estar* (*to be*)

There are two ways of saying *to be* in Spanish and the uses of each are clearly differentiated by the native speaker. Here are the Present tense forms of the two verbs:

ser			
soy		*I am*	
eres		*you are* (fam.)	
es	de Madrid	*you are* (form.), *he/she is*	*from Madrid*
somos		*we are*	
sois		*you are* (fam.)	
son		*you are* (form.), *they are*	

El, ella and **usted** in the singular and **ellos, ellas, ustedes** in the plural share the same forms. This is valid for all verbs.

él, ella, usted **es**   ellos, ellas, ustedes **son**

estar			
estoy		*I am*	
estás		*you are* (fam.)	
está	en Madrid	*you are, he/she is*	*in Madrid*
estamos		*we are*	
estáis		*you are* (fam.)	
están		*you are, they are*	

3   *Ser* is used:

(a)   To identify yourself or another person and to give personal information such as nationality, place of origin and occupation.

Soy Carlos Martínez.   *I'm Carlos Martínez.*
Soy español.   *I'm Spanish.*
Soy de Madrid.   *I'm from Madrid.*
Soy profesor.   *I'm a teacher.*

Note: For other uses of **de** refer to Unit 37.

Diálogo 1
A   Buenos días. ¿Usted es el señor Martínez?
B   Sí, soy Carlos Martínez.
A   ¿Es usted español?
B   Sí, soy español. Soy de Madrid.

buenos días   *good morning*   **sí**   *yes*

Note: **señor, señora, señorita** must be preceded by **el** or **la** in indirect address. Compare:

> Buenos días, señor Martínez. *Good morning, Mr Martínez.*
> ¿Usted es el señor Martínez? *Are you Mr Martínez?*

(b) To express an unchanging quality or characteristic.

> El hotel es excelente. *The hotel is excellent.*
> La comida es regular. *The food is not bad.*

Diálogo 2
A ¿Es bueno el Hotel Romántico?
B Sí, es excelente.
A ¿Y la comida?
B La comida es regular.

y *and*

(c) In impersonal expressions such as these:

> Es fácil. *It's easy.*
> Es difícil. *It's difficult.*

Diálogo 3
A ¿Es difícil el español para Vd.?
B No, es fácil.

el español *the Spanish language*
para Vd. *for you*

Note: For other uses of **para** refer to Unit 37.

PRACTIQUE

A *Complete these sentences with the correct form of* **ser**.
1 Ana . . . . . de Buenos Aires.
2 ¿Vd. . . . . . la señorita Rodríguez?
3 Nosotros . . . . . ingleses.
4 John y Sarah . . . . . americanos.
5 El señor García . . . . . un dentista excelente.
6 ¿ . . . . . fácil para Vd. el inglés?

el inglés *the English language*

B   *Look at Dialogue 1 above and make up a similar dialogue using these words*:

> buenas tardes (*good afternoon*)/la señora Carmen Pérez/española/de Sevilla.

4   *Estar* is used:

(a)   To refer to a state or condition which is temporary.

¿Cómo está Vd.?	*How are you?*
Estoy bien/contento.	*I'm fine/happy.*
El agua está caliente/fría.	*The water is hot/cold.*

Diálogo 4
A   Hola. ¿Cómo estás?
B   Estoy bien. ¿Y tú?
A   Muy bien, gracias.

hola   *hello*
muy bien   *very well*
gracias   *thank you*

(b)   To indicate location.

¿Dónde está el lavabo?	*Where is the toilet?*
Está allí.	*It's over there.*

Diálogo 5
A   Perdone. ¿Dónde está el lavabo, por favor?
B   Está allí.
A   Gracias.
B   De nada.

perdone   *excuse me (to call attention)*
por favor   *please*
de nada   *you're welcome*

(c)   To refer to civil status, although this can also be expressed with **ser**.

María está soltera.	*María is single.*
Pedro está casado.	*Pedro is married.*

Diálogo 6
A ¿Estás soltero o casado?
B Estoy soltero. ¿Y tú?
A Yo también.

o *or*
también *also*

(d) **Estar** contrasts with **ser** in sentences like these:

La ciudad **está** bonita.   *The city looks pretty.*
La ciudad **es** bonita.   *The city is pretty.*
Carlos **está** alegre.   *Carlos is happy (now).*
Silvia **es** alegre.   *Silvia is a happy person.*

For a more detailed study of the uses of **ser** and **estar** see the following Units: **ser**: Units 5, 13, 17, 25; **estar**: Units 3, 12, 20, 21.

PRACTIQUE
C *Complete these sentences with the correct form of* **estar**.
1 Ricardo . . . . muy bien.
2 ¿Dónde . . . . Málaga?
3 Las Islas Baleares . . . . en el Mediterráneo.
4 Mercedes y Joaquín . . . . casados.
5 ¿Cómo . . . . . (vosotros)?
6 (Nosotros) . . . . bien, gracias.

Islas Baleares *Balearic Islands*

D *Use the correct form of* **ser** *or* **estar** *according to the context.*
A Buenas tardes. (Yo) . . . . Joaquín Gallastegui.
¿Usted . . . . la señorita Santos?
B Sí, (yo) . . . . Mercedes Santos.
A ¿Cómo . . . . Vd., señorita?
B Bien, gracias. ¿Y usted?
A (Yo) . . . . muy bien, gracias.

E *Read these sentences.*
Me llamo Peter Brown.   *My name is Peter Brown.*
Soy inglés.   *I'm English.*

Soy de Londres.   *I'm from London.*
Estoy soltero.   *I'm single.*

Write similar sentences in Spanish about yourself. You may need one of these words:

irlandés/irlandesa *Irish*
galés/galesa *Welsh*
escocés/escocesa *Scottish*

americano/a *American*
australiano/a *Australian*
canadiense *Canadian*

4 Saying no and asking questions

1 Negative sentences

Negative sentences are formed by placing **no** before the verb. **No** translates into English as *no* and *not*.

¿**No** es Vd. inglesa?   *Aren't you English?*
No, no soy inglesa.   *No, I'm not English.*

Diálogo 1
A ¿Marta es argentina?
B No, no es argentina. Es española.
A ¿Es de Madrid?
B No, es de Salamanca.

PRACTIQUE
A *Make up negative and positive sentences.*
Ejemplo: ¿Es difícil el español? (fácil)
           No, no es difícil. Es fácil.
1 ¿Es español Pablo? (mexicano)
2 ¿Es bueno el hotel? (malo)
3 ¿Está en Barcelona María? (Bilbao)
4 ¿Estás casado? (soltero)
5 ¿Son buenos los restaurantes? (malos)
6 ¿Están en España Ana y Gloria? (Venezuela)

Other forms of negative such as **nadie** (*nobody/no-one*) and **nada** (*nothing*) will be found in Unit 11.

2 Interrogative sentences

There are four main ways of asking questions in Spanish.
(*a*) The simplest way to form a question is by using the same word order as in a statement but with a rising intonation. In writing, two

question marks must be used: one at the beginning of the sentence (¿) and one at the end (?).

¿Vd. es de Nueva York?	*Are you from New York?*
¿Eres americano?	*Are you American?*

(*b*) Questions can also be formed by inverting the word order and placing the subject after the verb.

Vds. son turistas.	*You are tourists.*
¿Son Vds. turistas?	*Are you tourists?*
Carmen es doctora.	*Carmen is a doctor.*
¿Es doctora Carmen?	*Is Carmen a doctor?*

(*c*) Another way of asking questions is by using the equivalent of phrases like *isn't it?, aren't you?, don't you?*. In Spanish these are **¿verdad?** and **¿no?** which are interchangeable and can be added to any statement to turn it into an interrogative sentence.

Barcelona es bonito, ¿verdad?	*Barcelona is nice, isn't it?*
Vd. es de Barcelona, ¿no?	*You are from Barcelona, aren't you?*

(*d*) As in English, questions can also be asked by using interrogative words.

¿Qué es?	*What is it?*
¿Qué significa?	*What does it mean?*
¿De qué color es?	*What colour is it?*
¿Cuánto es?	*How much is it?*
¿Cuánto cuesta(n)?	*How much does it (do they) cost?*
¿Cómo es?	*What is it like?*
¿Cuál es él?	*Which is him?*
¿Cuáles son?	*Which are they?*
¿Quién es?	*Who is it?*
¿Quiénes son?	*Who are they?*
¿De quién es?	*Whose is it?*
¿Cuántos son Vds.?	*How many are you?*
¿Dónde está?	*Where is it?*

¿De dónde eres?	*Where are you from?*
¿Adónde va Vd.?	*Where are you going to?*
¿Por qué?	*Why?*
¿Cuándo es?	*When is it?*

Two frequent phrases with **¿qué?** are **¿Qué tal?** and **¿Qué hay?** (*How are things?*). **¿Cómo?** is found in **¿Cómo se llama Vd.?** and **¿Cómo te llamas?** (*What's your name?*, formal and familiar, respectively). The answer to both is **Me llamo** (+ *name*).

Remember that all question words must carry an accent.

Diálogo 2
A   Hola. ¿De dónde eres?
B   Soy de Burgos.
      Tú eres de Avila, ¿verdad?
A   Sí, soy de Avila.

PRACTIQUE
B   *Turn the following statements into questions.*
Ejemplo: Berta está casada.
              ¿Está casada Berta?
1   Paco está en Segovia.
2   Paloma y Rocío son de Córdoba.
3   El camping El Sol es bueno.
4   Toledo es bonito.
5   Pepe está bien.
6   Ricardo y Cristóbal están solteros.

C   *Complete these sentences with an appropriate question word from section* (**d**) *above.*
1   ¿ . . . . es Vd.? Soy de Granada.
2   ¿ . . . . es? 10.000 pesetas.
3   ¿ . . . . está Sevilla? Está en Andalucía.
4   ¿ . . . . es el restaurante? Es excelente.
5   ¿ . . . . es Vd.? Soy Oscar Muñoz.
6   ¿ . . . . son ellos? Son Roberto y Cristina.

D   *Look at Dialogue 2 above and make up a similar conversation using the formal form* **usted**. *Use the name of other towns.*

5 Describing

1 Describing places, people and things

The verb most frequently used in describing places, people and things is **ser** (for its forms and a summary of its main uses see Unit 3).

Describing a place

Sitges está en Cataluña.	*Sitges is in Catalonia.*
Es una ciudad pequeña.	*It's a small town.*
Las playas **son** buenas.	*The beaches are good.*
Los hoteles no **son** caros.	*The hotels aren't expensive.*

Describing a person

Elena **es** sevillana.	*Elena is from Seville.*
Es alta y delgada.	*She's tall and slim.*
Es muy simpática.	*She's very nice.*

Describing a thing

El coche **es** francés.	*The car is French.*
Es bueno.	*It's good.*
Es grande.	*It's big.*
Es confortable.	*It's comfortable.*
Es moderno.	*It's modern.*

Diálogo 1

A   ¿Cómo es Cadaqués?
B   Ah, Cadaqués es un pueblo muy bonito.
A   ¿Son buenas las playas?
B   Son estupendas.
A   Y los hoteles, ¿son caros?
B   Sí, son bastante caros, pero el servicio es excelente.

un pueblo	*a small town*	**el servicio**	*service*
estupendo	*fantastic*	**pero**	*but*
bastante	*quite*		

PRACTIQUE

A *Read this description of a Spanish hotel.*

El Hotel Reina Sofía **es** un hotel de 5 (**cinco**) estrellas.
Es muy grande. Las habitaciones **son** confortables.   La comida
es excelente. El servicio **es** estupendo.

un hotel de 5 estrellas   *a 5-star hotel*
la habitación   *room*

Now use these words to write a description like the one above.

El Hotel Victoria—1 (**una**) estrella. Muy pequeño.
Las habitaciones—oscuras (*dark*).
La comida—regular.
El servicio—bastante malo.

B *Read this extract from a letter written by someone who is looking for a partner.*

... Me llamo
Miguel. Soy un
chico bajo y
delgado. Soy
interesante y
muy simpático...

bajo   *short*

Now use these words to write a similar paragraph about Julia: joven
(*young*), alta y delgada; bonita y simpática.

C *Complete these sentences with the correct form of* **ser**.
1 ¿Cómo . . . . las habitaciones?
2 El bar . . . . bastante malo.
3 Vosotros . . . . bastante altos.
4 Nosotros . . . . bajos.
5 ¿Cómo . . . . el coche?
6 Los coches franceses . . . . buenos.

2 Describing the weather

To describe the weather (**el tiempo**) Spanish uses the verb **hacer** which literally means to do or to make. French uses a similar construction with *faire*. You only need the 3rd person singular **hace** followed by a word descriptive of the weather.

¿Qué tiempo hace?	*What's the weather like?*
Hace (mucho) calor.	*It's (very) hot.*
Hace (bastante) frío.	*It's (quite) cold.*
Hace sol.	*It's sunny.*
Hace viento.	*It's windy.*
Hace (muy) buen tiempo.	*The weather is (very) good.*
Hace (muy) mal tiempo.	*The weather is (very) bad.*
¿Qué temperatura hace?	*What's the temperature?*
Hace 30 (treinta) grados.	*It's 30 degrees.*

Notice we use **mucho** (lit. *much, a lot*) before nouns, e.g. **calor, frío, sol, viento** and **muy** (*very*) before an adjective, e.g. **muy buen/mal (tiempo)**.

There are a few expressions which do not carry the verb **hacer**.

Llueve (llover)	*It rains (to rain)*
Está lloviendo.	*It's raining.*
Nieva (nevar)	*It snows (to snow)*
Está nevando.	*It's snowing.*

If we are referring to the climate (**el clima**) in general terms we may use the verb **ser**.

El clima (o el tiempo) es caluroso. *The climate (* or *weather) is warm.*

Es frío/fresco/templado. *It's cold fresh temperate.*

The above words are adjectives, not nouns.

Diálogo 2
A ¿Qué tiempo hace en Sevilla hoy?
B Hace mucho calor.
A ¿Qué temperatura hace?
B Hace 35 (treinta y cinco) grados.
A ¡Qué calor!

¡Qué calor! *How warm!*

PRACTIQUE

D *You are talking to a Spanish friend on the phone. He wants to know what the weather is like in your town today.*

Amigo ¿Qué tiempo hace hoy?

Vd. (*Say it's quite cold but it's sunny. Ask what the weather is like over there.*)

Amigo Aquí hace demasiado calor.

demasiado calor *too hot*

6 This, that, these and those

1 Demonstrative adjectives

In Spanish, demonstrative adjectives have masculine and feminine as well as singular and plural forms.

> **este** dormitorio (masc., sing.) *this bedroom*
> **esta** habitación (fem., sing.) *this room*
> **estos** dormitorios (masc., pl.) *these bedrooms*
> **estas** habitaciones (fem., pl.) *these rooms*
>
> **ese** baño (masc., sing.) *that bathroom*
> **esa** ducha (fem., sing.) *that shower*
> **esos** baños (masc., pl.) *those bathrooms*
> **esas** duchas (fem. pl.) *those showers*

That may also be translated as **aquel** when it refers to something further away.

> **aquel** jardín (masc., sing.) *that garden*
> **aquella** puerta (fem., sing.) *that door*
> **aquellos** jardines (masc., pl.) *those gardens*
> **aquellas** puertas (fem., pl.) *those doors*

2 Demonstrative pronouns

All the above words have been followed by nouns: **este dormitorio, ese baño, aquel jardín.** But they may also be used to refer to a noun without mentioning it specifically:

> ¿cuál? *which one?*
> éste *this one*

In this case they act as pronouns and they must carry an accent to differentiate them from the adjectives (except on capital letters).

¿Cuál es el autobús para La Coruña? ¿Este o ése? *Which is the*
bus for Corunna? This one or that one?
Es ése. Este es el autobús para Zaragoza. *It's that one. This is*
the bus for Zaragoza.

Diálogo
A ¿Es éste el barco para Mallorca?
B No, señora. El barco para Mallorca es aquél.
   Este es el de Ibiza.
A Gracias.
B De nada.

el barco *boat*

PRACTIQUE
A *Use* **este, esta, estos, estas,** *as appropriate.*
1 . . . . avión es muy confortable.
2 . . . . autobuses son muy rápidos.
3 . . . . barco es muy bonito.
4 . . . . islas son españolas.
5 ¿Cómo se llama . . . . estación?
6 . . . . playas son estupendas.

el avión *aeroplane*

B *Ask how much something costs. Use* **ese, esa, esos, esas,** *as*
appropriate.
Ejemplo: la(s) chaqueta(s) (*jacket(s)*)
          ¿Cuánto cuesta(n) esa(s) chaqueta(s)?
1 el vestido (*dress*)
2 los pantalones (*trousers*)
3 la camisa (*shirt*)
4 los zapatos (*shoes*)
5 las blusas (*blouses*)
6 el traje (*suit*)

C *Complete these questions with the correct form of* **éste o ése.**
Ejemplo: ¿El cheque para el hotel es . . . . ?
          ¿El cheque para el hotel es éste o ése?

28 *This, that, these and those*

1 ¿El dinero para la habitación es . . . . ?
2 ¿Los sellos para Inglaterra son . . . . ?
3 ¿Las postales de Toledo son . . . . ?
4 ¿La tarjeta para Juan es . . . . ?
5 ¿El paquete para Isabel es . . . . ?
6 ¿La carta de Enrique es . . . . ?

el dinero *money*   **el paquete** *parcel*
el sello *stamp*   **la carta** *letter*
la postal *postcard*   **Inglaterra** *England*
la tarjeta *card*

7 Expressing possession

1 Possessive adjectives

To express possession we may, as in English, use possessive adjectives. In Spanish they agree with the noun that they accompany.

(a) To say *my* use **mi** or **mis**.

mi amigo/amiga	*my friend (male/female)*
mis amigos/amigas	*my friends (male/female)*

(b) To say *your* in a familiar way use **tu** or **tus**.

tu hijo/hija	*your son/daughter*
tus hijos/hijas	*your sons (or children)/daughters*

(c) To say *your* in a formal way and to say *his, her* and *its* use **su** or **sus**.

su hermano/hermana	*your, his, her, brother/sister*
sus hermanos/hermanas	*your, his, her, brothers (or brothers and sisters)/sisters.*

The context will normally make it clear whether you are talking about *your, his* or *her*.

(d) To say *our* use **nuestro** or **nuestros** when the noun which follows is masculine and **nuestra** or **nuestras** when it is feminine.

masc.	nuestro primo	*our cousin*
	nuestros primos	*our cousins*
fem.	nuestra prima	*our cousin*
	nuestras primas	*our cousins*

(e) To say *your* in a familiar way when you are talking to more than one person use **vuestro** or **vuestros** when the noun which follows is masculine and **vuestra** or **vuestras** when it is feminine.

30   *Expressing possession*

masc.	vuestro abuelo	*your grandfather*
	vuestros abuelos	*your grandparents*
fem.	vuestra abuela	*your grandmother*
	vuestras abuelas	*your grandmothers*

(**f**) To say *your* in a formal way when you are talking to more than one person and to say *their* use **su** or **sus**.

| su tío/tía | *your, their uncle/aunt* |
| sus tíos/tías | *your, their uncles/aunts* |

Diálogo 1: Mucho gusto (*Pleased to meet you*)
A   Hola Antonio, ¿qué tal?
B   Bien, gracias.
A   Este es Carlos, mi marido.
B   Hola, mucho gusto.
C   Encantado.

encantado   *pleased to meet you*   **el marido**   *husband*

Diálogo 2: Mi pasaporte, por favor (*My passport, please*)
Señorita   Buenos días. Mi pasaporte, por favor.
Recepcionista   ¿Es éste su pasaporte, señorita?
Señorita   No, este pasaporte es francés.
                   Mi pasaporte es británico.

el pasaporte   *passport*   **británico**   *British*

PRACTIQUE
A   *Answer each of these questions in the negative using the word in brackets in your reply.*
Ejemplo: ¿Es éste su pasaporte?   (británico)
          No, mi pasaporte es británico.
1 ¿Es ésta su cámara?   (japonesa)
2 ¿Son éstos sus zapatos?   (negros)
3 ¿Es ésta su radio?   (grande)
4 ¿Es éste su coche?   (un Seat)
5 ¿Son éstos sus pantalones?   (marrones)
6 ¿Son éstas sus postales?   (de Madrid)

japonés   *Japanese*   **marrón**   *brown*
negro   *black*

B *Play your part in this conversation.*

A ¿Están ustedes con sus hijos en España?

B (*No, our children are in England. I'm here with my husband/wife. Are your children here?*)

A Sí, ellos están aquí.

B (*Where are you from?*)

A Somos de Madrid. ¿Y en qué parte de Inglaterra está su casa?

B (*Our house is in London.*)

con *with*
¿en qué parte? *in what part?*

2 Expressing possession with '*de*'

Another frequent way of expressing possession in Spanish is by using phrases such as these:

El novio de María.	*Maria's boyfriend.*
El pasaporte de la Sra Brown.	*Mrs Brown's passport.*
El niño del Sr Johnson.	*Mr Johnson's child*

For other uses of the preposition **de** refer to Unit 37.

PRACTIQUE

C *Say who each of the following belongs to by using the words in brackets in your reply.*

Ejemplo: ¿De quién es esa casa?   (María)
        Es la casa de María.

1 ¿De quién es ese coche?   (Sr Pérez)
2 ¿De quién es esa habitación?   (Carlos)
3 ¿De quién son esos zapatos?   (mi hija)
4 ¿De quién es esa chaqueta?   (Laura)
5 ¿De quién son esos pantalones?   (Jorge)
6 ¿De quién es ese chico?   (Sra Ramírez)

3 Possessive Pronouns

Possession can also be expressed by means of possessive pronouns. These must also agree with the nouns that they accompany.

(*a*)   To say *mine* use **mío(s)** or **mía(s)**

> *masc.*
> | | |
> |---|---|
> | Este traje es mío. | *This suit is mine.* |
> | Estos calcetines son míos. | *These socks are mine.* |
>
> *fem.*
> | | |
> |---|---|
> | Esta falda es mía. | *This skirt is mine.* |
> | Estas medias son mías. | *These stockings are mine.* |

If the noun is understood we may simply use phrases like these: **el mío, los míos, la mía, las mías** (*mine*), depending on whether the noun referred to is masculine or feminine, singular or plural.

> | | |
> |---|---|
> | Este traje es mío. | *This suit is mine.* |
> | Este es el mío. | *This is mine.* |

(*b*)   To say *yours* in a familiar way use **tuyo(s)** or **tuya(s)**.

> *masc.*
> | | |
> |---|---|
> | ¿Es tuyo este impermeable? | *Is this raincoat yours?* |
> | ¿Son tuyos estos cigarrillos? | *Are these cigarettes yours?* |
>
> *fem.*
> | | |
> |---|---|
> | ¿Es tuya esta cartera? | *Is this briefcase yours?* |
> | ¿Son tuyas estas cerillas? | *Are these matches yours?* |

(*c*)   To say *yours* in a formal way and to say *his*, *hers*, *its*, use **suyo(s)** or **suya(s)**.

> *masc.*
> | | |
> |---|---|
> | ¿Es suyo este maletín? | *Is this briefcase yours?* |
> | ¿Son suyos estos cheques? | *Are these cheques yours?* |
>
> *fem.*
> | | |
> |---|---|
> | ¿Es suya esta maleta? | *Is this suitcase yours?* |
> | ¿Son suyas estas bolsas? | *Are these bags yours?* |

To avoid ambiguity and clarify whether you mean *yours*, *his* or *hers* you may use phrases like these:

> | | |
> |---|---|
> | ¿Es de él este diario? | *Is this newspaper his?* |
> | ¿Es de ella esta revista? | *Is this magazine hers?* |

(*d*)   To say *ours* use **nuestro(s)** or **nuestra(s)**.

masc.

Este equipaje es nuestro.	*This luggage is ours.*
Estos billetes son nuestros.	*These tickets are ours.*

fem.

Esta caja es nuestra.	*This box is ours.*
Estas maletas son nuestras.	*These suitcases are ours.*

(*e*)   To say *yours* in a familiar way when you are talking to more than one person use **vuestro(s)** or **vuestra(s)**.

masc.

¿Es vuestro este apartamento?	*Is this apartment yours?*
¿Son vuestros estos niños?	*Are these children yours?*

fem.

¿Es vuestra esta casa?	*Is this house yours?*
¿Son vuestras estas niñas?	*Are these girls yours?*

(*f*)   To say *yours* in a formal way when talking to more than one person and to say *theirs* use **suyo(s)** or **suya(s)**.

masc.

Este dinero es suyo.	*This money is yours.*
Estos documentos son suyos.	*These documents are yours.*

fem.

Esta llave es suya.	*This key is yours.*
Estas gafas son suyas.	*These glasses are yours.*

To avoid ambiguity and clarify whether you mean *yours* or *theirs* you may use phrases like these:

Esta llave es de ustedes.	*This key is yours.*
Esta llave es de ellos.	*This key is theirs.*

Diálogo 3: ¿Esta maleta es suya? (*Is this suitcase yours?*)

A   ¿Esta maleta es suya?

B   No, no es mía. La mía es marrón.
      Esa es la maleta del señor Rodríguez.

A   Perdone.

PRACTIQUE

D   *Express possession as in the example.*

Ejemplo: Su habitación es la número 10. (15)
      La mía es la número 15.

1 Su maleta es negra.   (marrón)
2 Su impermeable es americano.   (inglés)
3 Sus cigarrillos son españoles.   (franceses)
4 Su equipaje es éste.   (aquél)
5 Su casa es pequeña.   (grande)
6 Sus amigos son de Andalucía.   (de Cataluña)

el número   *number*

E   *Complete these sentences with the appropriate possessive pronoun.*

1 Estas maletas no son . . .   vuestros
2 ¿Es . . . este pasaporte, señorita?   nuestra
3 ¿Estos chicos son . . . ?   suyo
4 'Carlos, esta chaqueta es . . .'   vuestra
5 ¿Es . . . esta casa?   la tuya
6 Esta llave no es . . . Nosotros estamos   las nuestras
   en la habitación 20.

4   Possession with *tener*

Possession can also be expressed with the verb **tener** (*to have*). See
Unit 8, page 35.

8 I have . . . , you have . . .

Tener

(*a*) The Spanish word **tener** normally corresponds to the English verb *to have*, as in **tengo una cita** (*I have an appointment*). However, in certain contexts **tener** translates into English as *to be* as in **tengo veinte años** (*I'm twenty years old*). The Present tense forms of **tener** are:

tengo	*I have*
tienes	*you have* (fam.)
tiene	*you have, he/she/it has*
tenemos	*we have*
tenéis	*you have* (fam.)
tienen	*you/they have*

(*b*) **Tener** expresses possession.
¿Cuánto dinero tiene Vd.? *How much money have you got?*
Tengo cien libras. *I have one hundred pounds.*

(*c*) It may express availability.
¿Tiene Vd. una habitación? *Have you got a room?*
No tengo. *I haven't got (any).*

(*d*) It may express physical discomfort.
¿Qué tienes? *What's the matter with you?*
   (Lit. What have you got?)
Tengo dolor de cabeza. *I have a headache.*
Tengo dolor de estómago. *I have a stomach-ache.*
Tengo fiebre. *I have a temperature.*

(*e*) It may be used to ask the time or to ask for a light.
¿Tienes hora? *Have you got the time?*
¿Tienes fuego? *Have you got a light?*

(*f*)   It may be used to say that you have an appointment, a meeting, a party, etc.

Tengo una cita.   *I have an appointment.*
Tenemos una reunión.   *We have a meeting.*
Tienen una fiesta.   *They have a party.*

(*g*)   **Tener** is also used to ask and answer questions about age, in which case it translates into English as *to be*.

¿Cuántos años tienes tú?   *How old are you?*
Tengo 30 años.   *I'm 30 years old.*

(*h*)   Here is a list of expressions in which **tener** is equivalent to the English verb *to be*.

Tener hambre	*to be hungry*	Tengo hambre.
Tener sed	*to be thirsty*	Tengo sed.
Tener frío	*to be cold*	Tengo frío.
Tener calor	*to be warm*	Tengo calor.
Tener razón	*to be right*	Tiene Vd. razón.
Tener cuidado	*to be careful*	El tiene mucho cuidado.

2   *Tener que*

Tener que + infinitive means *to have to do something*.

Tiene que ser hoy.   *It has to be today.*
Tengo que estar allí pronto.   *I have to be there soon.*

Diálogo 1: ¿Qué tienes? (*What's the matter with you?*)
A   ¿Qué tienes?
B   Tengo dolor de estómago.
A   ¿Tienes fiebre también?
B   Sí, tengo un poco de fiebre.

Diálogo 2: ¿Tiene Vd. una mesa? (*Have you got a table?*)
A   ¿Tiene Vd. una mesa para cuatro?
B   Un momento, por favor.
    Lo siento, sólo tengo una para dos.
A   ¡Qué pena! Buenas noches.
B   Buenas noches, señor.

lo siento   *I'm sorry*   ¡**qué pena!**   *what a pity*
sólo   *only*   **buenas noches**   *good night*

PRACTIQUE

A   *Complete these sentences with the correct form of* **tener.**

1 ¿Cuántas maletas . . . tú?
2 (Yo) no . . . equipaje.
3 (Nosotros) . . . pasaportes británicos.
4 ¿Qué pasaporte . . . ella?
5 (Vosotros) . . . un apartamento muy bonito.
6 ¿ . . . Vd. fuego, por favor?

B   *Ask whether the following is available.*
Ejemplo: Una habitación doble   (*a double room*)
          ¿Tiene Vd. una habitación doble?

1 Una habitación individual   (*a single room*)
2 Una mesa para dos   (*a table for two*)
3 Periódicos ingleses   (*English newspapers*)
4 Cambio   (*change*)
5 La cuenta   (*the bill*)
6 Mi billete   (*my ticket*)

C   *Match each of the following spaces with a verb selected from the list.*

1 (Vosotros) . . . razón.   tienes
2 (Yo) . . . mucho calor.   tiene
3 ¿ . . . frío (tú)?   tengo
4 (Nosotros) . . . mucha hambre.   tienen
5 ¿ Cuántos años . . . Vd.?   tenemos
6 Cristóbal y María . . . mucha sed. tenéis

D   *Answer these questions about yourself.*

1 ¿Qué pasaporte tiene Vd.?
2 ¿Cuántos años tiene Vd.?
3 ¿Tiene Vd. hermanos/hijos?
  ¿Cuántos hermanos/hijos tiene?
4 ¿Tiene Vd. una casa o un piso (*a flat*)?
5 ¿Cuántas habitaciones tiene la casa/el piso?

9 Making comparisons

1 Comparatives

(*a*) In English we normally make comparisons by adding *-er* to some adjectives or by using the word *more* in front of an adverb, a noun or an adjective: *nicer, more beautiful, more difficult*. In Spanish, to compare one thing with another we use the word **más**. In comparative sentences the Spanish equivalent of *than* is **que**.

> El pollo es **más** barato **que** la carne de vaca. *Chicken is cheaper than beef.*
> El vino es **más** caro **que** la cerveza. *Wine is more expensive than beer.*

(*b*) **Bueno** (*good*), **bien** (*well*), **malo** (*bad*), **mal** (*bad, badly*) do not follow the above rule in forming their comparatives:

bueno: bien   **mejor** (*better*)
malo: mal   **peor** (*worse*)

> Esta carne está **mejor**. *This meat is better.*
> La comida aquí es **peor**. *The food here is worse.*

(*c*) **Grande** (*big*) and **pequeño** (*small*) become **mayor** (*larger, older*) and **menor** (*smaller, younger*), but also **más grande** and **más pequeño** when referring to size.

> Mi hermano es **mayor**. *My brother is older.*
> Mi casa es **más grande**. *My house is larger.*

(*d*) To express equality or inequality between two things we use **tan . . . como**.

> El pescado (no) es **tan** caro **como** la carne. *Fish is (not) as expensive as meat.*
> Mi café (no) está **tan** frío **como** el tuyo. *My coffee is (not) as cold as yours.*

(*e*)   If the comparison involves not an adjective but a noun, we use **tanto . . . como** or one of its forms: **tanto, tanta, tantos, tantas**, depending on the gender (masculine and feminine) and number (singular and plural) of the noun referred to.

> El bebe **tanto** té **como** yo.   *He drinks as much tea as I (do).*
> Ella come **tanta** carne **como** tú.   *She eats as much meat as you (do).*
> Aquí no tienen **tantas** verduras (o legumbres).   *They don't have as many vegetables here.*

2 Superlatives

To say things like *the nicest, the most beautiful,* Spanish uses the word **más** preceded by **el, la, los** or **las,** depending on the gender and number of what you want to compare.

> Aquel camarero es **el más** simpático.   *That waiter is the nicest.*
> Esa cafetería es **la más** agradable.   *That café is the most pleasant.*

Diálogo 1: **Aquéllas son más caras** (*Those are more expensive*)
A   ¿Cuánto cuestan estas naranjas? (*oranges*)
B   Cien pesetas el kilo.
A   ¿Y aquéllas?
B   Aquéllas son más caras, pero son mejores que éstas. Cuestan ciento veinte pesetas.

Diálogo 2: **Es el mejor bar**   (*It's the best bar*)
A   Ese es el Bar Santa María. Es el mejor bar de la ciudad y el más agradable.
B   ¿Es tan barato como el Bar Don Pepe?
A   No, no es tan barato, pero el servicio es excelente.

PRACTIQUE

A   *Look at Dialogue 1 above and make up similar conversations using the following words. See Appendix 1 on p. 155 for a list of numbers.*

Fruta o verdura (*fruit or vegetable*)	*Pts.* (*pesetas*)
(las) manzanas (*apples*)	70–90

(las) peras	(*pears*)	60–75
(las) patatas	(*potatoes*)	40–50
(las) lechugas	(*lettuce*)	30–45
(los) tomates	(*tomatoes*)	90–130

B *Make up sentences with* **el, la, los** *or* **las . . . más,** *as appropriate.*
Ejemplo: El autoservicio Mediterráneo—rápido.
El autoservicio Mediterráneo es el más rápido.
The Mediterráneo is the fastest self-service.
1 El Club Montserrat – confortable.
2 La Pensión Bellavista – barata.
3 El Bar Paco y el Bar Gustavo – tranquilos.
4 El Restaurante Gracia – agradable.
5 La Cafetería Roma y la Cafetería Rosa – grandes.
6 El Café Los Artistas – antiguo.

la pensión *boarding-house*   **antiguo** *old*
tranquilo *quiet*

C *Complete these sentences with* **tanto, -a, -os, -as . . . como,** *as appropriate.*
Ejemplo: Tengo . . . sed . . . tú.
Tengo tanta sed como tú.
1 Benidorm tiene . . . turistas . . . Torremolinos.
2 En Londres hace . . . frío . . . en París.
3 Tienes . . . dinero . . : yo.
4 Tienen . . . amigos . . . nosotros.
5 No tengo . . . maletas tú.
6 Mi casa tiene . . . habitaciones . . . la tuya.

10 There is, there are

1 *Hay*

To say *there is* or *there are* Spanish uses the single word **hay**. It is also used in interrogative sentences where it translates as *is there?* or *are there?*

> **Hay** muchas tiendas en esta calle.   *There are many shops in this street.*
>
> ¿**Hay** un supermercado por aquí?   *Is there a supermarket around here?*
>
> En este pueblo no **hay** supermercados.   *In this village there are no supermarkets.*

Diálogo 1: **Hay una en la esquina** (*There is one at the corner*)
A   Buenos días. ¿Hay una panadería por aquí?
B   Sí, hay una en la esquina.
A   Muchas gracias.
B   De nada.

la panadería   *baker's*

Diálogo 2: **Arriba hay dos** (*There are two upstairs*)
A   Perdone, ¿hay teléfonos en esta tienda?
B   Sí, arriba hay dos.
A   Gracias.
B   De nada.

PRACTIQUE

A   *Look at Dialogue 1 above and make up similar conversations using the following words.*

1 Una farmacia (*chemist's*) – en la plaza.
2 Una carnicería (*butcher's*) – en la Calle Mayor.
3 Un hospital – en la Avenida Libertad.

42   *There is, there are*

B   *Look at the facilities in this hotel and answer the following questions using* **Hay** . . . *or* **No hay** . . .

HOTEL EL CID
Restaurante Sí (1)
Bar Sí (2)
Piscina Sí (1)
Televisión Sí
Teléfono No
Aparcamiento No

Ejemplo:
¿Hay restaurante en el hotel?
Sí, hay uno.
1 ¿Hay bar?
2 ¿Hay piscina?
3 ¿Hay televisión en las habitaciones?
4 ¿Hay teléfono en las habitaciones?
5 ¿Hay aparcamiento en el hotel?

la piscina   *swimming pool*
el aparcamiento   *parking*

2   *Había/habrá*

Hay forms part of the auxiliary verb **haber** (*to have*). To say *there was* or *there were* we normally use the word **había**. To say *there will be* **hay** becomes **habrá**.

> **Había** una fiesta en casa de Juan.   *There was a party at Juan's house.*
> En la fiesta **había** veinte personas.   *There were twenty people at the party.*
> Mañana **habrá** una reunión.   *Tomorrow there will be a meeting.*
> **Habrá** muchas personas (o mucha gente) en la reunión.   *There will be many people at the meeting.*

Note: **gente** (*people*) is not normally used in the plural, therefore if we want to specify the number of people we have to use the word **persona,** e.g. *tres personas.*

C   *Play your part in this conversation.*
   A ¿Había mucha gente en la fiesta?
   B (*Yes, there were fifteen people*)
   A ¿Había amigos tuyos?

B (*Yes, there were two friends of mine, Alberto and Marisol.*)
A ¿Había mucha comida?
B (*Yes, there was a lot of food.*)

Note: For other uses of the prepositions **en** and **por**, seen in many of the examples in this chapter, refer to Unit 37.

11 Something, somebody, nothing, nobody

1 *Algo – nada*

Algo translates into English as *something* or *anything* while **nada** means *nothing*. Except for emphasis both words normally go after the verb.

> ¿Tiene Vd. **algo** que declarar? *Have you got anything to declare?*
> No tengo **nada** que declarar. *I have nothing to declare.*

Two frequent expressions with **algo** and **nada** are:

> ¿**Algo** más? *Anything else?*
> **Nada** más, gracias. *Nothing else, thank you.*

Note the use of the double negative **No** tengo **nada** (*I have nothing*), which is a standard Spanish construction, as the word **no** cannot be omitted.

Algo and **nada** may be used before an uncountable noun to indicate quantity. In this case they must be followed by the preposition **de**.

> ¿Tienes **algo de** dinero? *Have you got some money?*
> No tengo **nada de** dinero. *I have no money.*

2 *Alguien – nadie*

To say *somebody* or *anybody* we use the word **alguien**, while **nadie** means *nobody* or *no one*. Both words may be used before or after the verb.

¿Hay **alguien** allí?   *Is there anybody there?*
No hay **nadie**.   *There's no one.*

¿**Alguien** tiene un cigarrillo?   *Does anybody have a cigarette?*
Nadie tiene cigarrillos.   *Nobody has cigarettes.*

Notice again the double negative when **nadie** goes after the verb.

No hay **nadie**.   *There is nobody.*

3 *Alguno – ninguno*

To say *some (of them)* or *any (of them)* use **alguno** if the word
referred to is masculine and **alguna** if it is feminine. Both words have
plural forms: **algunos, algunas.**

¿Tiene Vd. **alguna** habitación?   *Have you got any room?*
¿Tiene Vd. **alguna**?   *Have you got any?*

Algunas de las habitaciones son tranquilas.   *Some of the rooms
    are quiet.*
Algunas son tranquilas.   *Some are quiet.*

The negative forms **ninguno** and **ninguna** may be translated as *no*, or
none (of them).

Ninguna habitación tiene vista al mar.   *No room has a sea view.*
Ninguna tiene vista al mar.   *None of them has a sea view.*

Before a masculine singular noun **alguno** and **ninguno** drop the **-o** and
become **algún** and **ningún.**

¿Hay **algún** banco por aquí?   *Is there any bank around here?*
Por aquí no hay **ningún** banco.   *There isn't any bank around
    here.*

Alguno and **ninguno** may also refer to people.

¿**Alguno** de vosotros tiene cambio?   *Do any of you have change?*
Ninguno de ellos habla castellano.   *None of them speaks
    Spanish (or Castilian).*

Note: In certain parts of Spain (e.g., Catalonia, Basque Country)
you'll hear the word **castellano** more often than the word **español**.

Diálogo 1: No tenemos ninguna (*We haven't got any*)
A   Buenas tardes. ¿Tiene alguna mesa libre?
B   Lo siento, no tenemos ninguna.
A   En aquella mesa no hay nadie.
B   Sí, pero está reservada.

está reservada   *it is reserved*

Diálogo 2: No hay nada (*There is nothing*)
A   ¿Hay algo interesante en la televisión esta tarde?
B   No hay nada.
A   ¡Qué lástima!

esta tarde   *this evening*
¡qué lástima!   *what a pity!*

PRACTIQUE
A   *Answer each of the questions in the negative.*
Ejemplo: ¿Hay alguien en casa?
          No hay nadie.
1   ¿Hay **algo** en esta maleta?
2   ¿Tiene usted **algo** que declarar?
3   ¿Tienes **algo** de dinero?
4   ¿Hay **alguien** en la habitación?
5   ¿Hay **algún** supermercado por aquí?
6   ¿Hay **alguna** farmacia por aquí?

B   *Complete each sentence with an appropriate word from the list:*
nada, nadie, ningún, alguna, alguien, algo.
1   Esta noche no hay . . . . . . programa interesante.
2   ¿Hay . . . . . . carta para el Sr Paz?
3   No tengo . . . . . . de dinero.
4   '¿Ana está con . . . . . . ?' – 'Sí, está con un amigo.'
5   '¿ . . . . . . más, señor?' – 'Nada más, gracias.'
6   '¿Alguien tiene fuego?' – 'No, ...'

esta noche   *tonight*

4 *Otro, otra, otros, otras*

To say (*the*) *other*, (*the*) *others* or *another* we use **otro** or one of its forms, depending on the gender (masculine or feminine) and number (singular or plural) of the word it refers to.

El otro disco es mejor.	*The other record is better.*
Los otros son mejores.	*The others are better.*
¿Tienes **otra** cinta?	*Have you got another tape?*
No tengo **otras**.	*I don't have others.*

5 *Todo, toda, todos, todas*

To say *every*(*thing*), *all* or *whole* we use **todo** or one of its forms, depending on the gender and number of the word it refers to.

Todo está listo.	*Everything is ready.*
Toda la gente está ahí.	*All the people are there.*
Todos están abajo.	*They are all downstairs.*
Llueve **todo** el día.	*It rains the whole day.*
Llueve **todos** los días.	*It rains every day.*

PRACTIQUE

C *Answer each of these questions in the negative using* **otro** *or one of its forms.*

Ejemplo: ¿Tiene una chaqueta más barata?
          No, no tengo otra.

1 ¿Tiene unos zapatos más grandes?
2 ¿Tiene una cartera mejor?
3 ¿Tiene blusas más pequeñas?
4 ¿Tiene un traje más barato?

D *Complete these sentences with* **todo, toda, todos** *or* **todas**.

1 El Sr Ruiz está en casa . . . la tarde.
2 . . . mis amigos están aquí.
3 Tengo . . . el dinero.
4 . . . las noches hace mucho frío.

12 Indicating location

1 Use of *estar*

To indicate location we normally use the verb **estar**, *to be*. (For its forms and a summary of its main uses see Unit 3, pp. 14–17.)

> ¿Dónde **está** la oficina de Correos? *Where is the post-office?*
> Correos **está** al lado del banco. *The post-office is next to the bank.*
>
> ¿Dónde **están** los servicios? *Where are the toilets?*
> **Están** ahí, a la derecha. *They are there, on the right.*
>
> ¿Dónde **están** las llaves? *Where are the keys?*
> **Están** sobre la mesa. *They are on the table.*
>
> ¿Dónde **está** tu familia? *Where is your family?*
> **Están** de vacaciones en España. *They are on holiday in Spain*

2 Words of location

Here is a list of the most frequent words and phrases used in expressing location.

al lado (de)	*next (to)*	encima (de)	*above, on top*
alrededor (de)	*around*	enfrente (de)	*opposite, in front*
a la derecha	*on the right*	fuera (de)	*out, outside*
a la izquierda	*on the left*	junto a	*next to*
cerca (de)	*near*	lejos (de)	*far (from)*
debajo (de)	*under*	sobre	*on, on top*
delante (de)	*in front (of)*	el norte	*north*
dentro (de)	*inside*	el sur	*south*
detrás (de)	*behind*	el este	*east*
en	*in, on, at*	el oeste	*west*

Diálogo 1: Al lado de Correos (*Next to the post-office*)

A ¿Dónde está la Telefónica, por favor?
B Está en la Plaza España, al lado de Correos.
A ¿Está lejos?
B No, está cerca.
A Muchas gracias.

la (Compañía) Telefónica *the Telephone Company*

Diálogo 2: Enfrente de la iglesia (*Opposite the church*)

A Perdone, ¿dónde está el museo?
B Está en la Calle Santander, enfrente de la iglesia.
A ¿La Calle Santander . . . ?
B La Calle Santander está aquí a la izquierda.
A Gracias.
B De nada.

el museo *museum*

3 Distance

To indicate distance you must use the preposition **a**.

El museo está **a** dos calles de aquí. *The museum is two streets from here.*
El parque está **a** diez minutos. *The park is ten minutes away.*
Toledo está **a** 70 km (kilómetros) de Madrid. *Toledo is 70 km from Madrid.*

PRACTIQUE

A *Ask and give directions using these words and phrases.*
Ejemplo: el camping/detrás/la estación.
           ¿Dónde está el camping?
           Está detrás de la estación.
1 La estación de autobuses/enfrente/Correos.
2 La estación de servicio/al lado/el hospital.
3 Los servicios/detrás/el ayuntamiento.
4 El garaje/junto a/la estación de servicio.
5 La catedral/la plaza.
6 El museo/cerca/la catedral.

la estación de autobuses *bus-station*
la estación de servicio *service-station*
el ayuntamiento *town-hall*

B *Answer these questions using the suggested answers in brackets.*
Ejemplo: ¿Dónde está Sevilla? (*In the south of Spain*)
        Sevilla está en el sur de España.
1 ¿Dónde está Bilbao? (*In the north of Spain*)
2 ¿Dónde está Sitges? (*35 km. from Barcelona*)
3 ¿Dónde está Valencia? (*In the east of Spain*)
4 ¿Dónde están las Islas Baleares? (*In the Mediterranean*)
5 ¿Dónde está Fuengirola? (*An hour* (una hora) *from Málaga*)
6 ¿Dónde está el ayuntamiento? (*Three streets from here*)

C *Answer these questions about yourself.*
1 ¿En qué ciudad está su casa/piso?
2 ¿En qué parte de la ciudad está?
3 ¿Dónde está su familia?

Note: For a comprehensive study of prepositions such as **en, de, a,** refer to Unit 37.

13 Asking and telling the time

1 Asking the time

There are two main ways of asking the time in Spanish. The most frequent expression uses the verb **ser,** *to be*. (For its forms and main uses see Unit 3, pp. 14–16).

> ¿Qué hora **es**?   *What time is it?*

But you can also use **tener,** *to have*, as in English (for its forms and main uses see Unit 8, pp. 34–6).

> ¿**Tiene** hora?   *Have you got the time?*

2 Telling the time

(*a*) To tell the time you must use **ser**.

Es la una   **Son** las tres menos cuarto.

Es la una y cuarto.   **Son** las cuatro y veinte.

Son las dos.   **Son** las cinco menos diez.

Son las dos y media.   **Son** las doce.

Note that we use the singular form **es** when the phrase contains the word **una**.

(*b*)   To say *in the morning, in the afternoon, at night,* in this context, we use the phrases **de la mañana, de la tarde, de la noche**.

> Son las tres **de** la tarde.   *It's 3 o'clock in the afternoon.*
> Son las once **de** la noche.   *It's 11 o'clock at night.*

Note: In other contexts we use the preposition **por** instead of **de**.

> La reunión es **por** la mañana.   *The meeting is in the morning.*
> **Por** la noche hace frío.   *It's cold at night.*

Diálogo 1: ¿Qué hora es? (*What's the time?*)
A   Perdone, ¿qué hora es?
B   Son las seis y cuarto.
A   ¡Las seis y cuarto! Hasta luego.

hasta luego   *see you later*

Diálogo 2: ¿Tiene hora? (*Have you got the time?*)
A   ¿Tiene hora, por favor?
B   Sí, es la una y media.
A   Gracias.

PRACTIQUE

A *Practise asking and telling the time.*
Ejemplo: ¿Qué hora es? o ¿Tiene hora?   (2.15)
        Son las dos y cuarto.

(1) 1.10.   (4) 5.00.   (7) 9.50
(2) 1.20.   (5) 6.40.   (8) 10.10
(3) 4.30   (6) 7.15.   (9) 11.45

3   At what time?

To ask at what time something is due to take place we use the phrase
¿A qué hora?

> **¿A qué hora** es la fiesta?   *What time is the party?*
> Es a las nueve.   *It's at 9.00.*

PRACTIQUE

B *Say at what time each of the following will take place.*
Ejemplo: ¿A qué hora es la reunión?   (11.30)
        Es a las once y media.

1 ¿A qué hora es la excursión?   (8.00)
2 ¿A qué hora es la clase?   (10.45)
3 ¿A qué hora es la cena?   (9.15)
4 ¿A qué hora es el desayuno?   (8.30)

la clase   *class*
la cena   *dinner*
el desayuno   *breakfast*

14 Talking about the present

1 Verbs – the three categories

According to the ending of the infinitive (or dictionary form of the verb), Spanish verbs may be grouped into three main categories: **-ar** (or 1st conjugation), **-er** (or 2nd conjugation) and **-ir** (or 3rd conjugation) verbs.

Ejemplos:

-ar	trabaj**ar**	*to work*
-er	com**er**	*to eat*
-ir	viv**ir**	*to live*

2 Regular verbs

Most Spanish verbs are regular, that is, they change in a fixed way according to person (three singular and three plural forms), tense (e.g. Present tense) and mood (e.g. indicative or subjunctive; see Unit 33 for an introduction to the subjunctive).

Ejemplos:
Trabaj**o** aquí.   *I work here.*
(1st person singular of the Present tense indicative)
Trabaj**amos** en Madrid.   *We work in Madrid.*
(1st person plural of the Present tense indicative)
Trabaj**an** mucho.   *They work a lot.*
(3rd person plural of the Present tense indicative)

Verbs which do not follow the fixed pattern are called irregular, e.g. **ser** (Unit 3, pp. 14–15), **estar** (Unit 3, pp. 14–17), **tener** (Unit 8, pp. 35–6).

3 Present tense – formation

(*a*) 1st conjugation: -**ar** verbs.

Ejemplo: **trabajar** *to work*

trabaj**o**	*I work*	trabaj**amos**	*we work*
trabaj**as**	*you work* (fam.)	trabaj**áis**	*you work* (fam.)
trabaj**a**	*you work, he/she works*	trabaj**an**	*you/they work*

(*b*) 2nd conjugation: -**er** verbs.

Ejemplo: **comer** *to eat*

com**o**	*I eat*	com**emos**	*we eat*
com**es**	*you eat* (fam.)	com**éis**	*you eat* (fam.)
com**e**	*you eat, he/she eats*	com**en**	*you/they eat*

(*c*) 3rd conjugation: -**ir** verbs.

Ejemplo: **vivir** *to live*

viv**o**	*I live*	viv**imos**	*we live*
viv**es**	*you live* (fam.)	viv**ís**	*you live* (fam.)
viv**e**	*you live, he/she lives*	viv**en**	*you/they live*

(*d*) Here are some more examples of verbs which are regular in the Present:

bajar	*to go down*	llamar	*to call*
comprar	*to buy*	llegar	*to arrive*
cenar	*to have dinner*	mirar	*to look, to watch*
contestar	*to answer*	tardar	*to take time*
desayunar	*to have breakfast*	terminar	*to finish*
estudiar	*to study*	viajar	*to travel*
hablar	*to speak*	visitar	*to visit*
aprender	*to learn*	abrir	*to open*
beber	*to drink*	escribir	*to write*
comprender	*to understand*	permitir	*to allow*
creer	*to think*	recibir	*to receive*
responder	*to answer*	subir	*to go up*

4 Uses of the Present tense

As in English, to talk about present actions and about things which are generally true, we use the Present tense.

Trabajo en una oficina.	*I work in an office.*
Como en una cafetería.	*I eat in a café.*
Vivo en un apartamento.	*I live in an apartment.*

Diálogo 1: ¿Habla Vd. español? (*Do you speak Spanish?*)
A ¿Habla Vd. español?
B Sí, hablo español y algo de francés. ¿Vd. habla inglés?
B No, no hablo nada de inglés.

Diálogo 2: ¿Dónde trabajas? (*Where do you work?*)
A ¿Dónde trabajas?
B Trabajo en un hospital. Soy médico. ¿Y tú?
A Yo trabajo en un instituto. Soy profesora.

el médico *doctor*
el instituto *secondary school*

Diálogo 3: ¿Qué escribes? (*What are you writing?*)
A ¿Qué escribes?
B Escribo una carta a mis padres.
A ¿Dónde viven?
B Viven en Mallorca.

PRACTIQUE

A *Change the infinitive into the correct form of the Present tense.*
Ejemplo: Ana (*vivir*) en Málaga.
          Ana vive en Málaga.
1 Mis padres (*viajar*) a España todos los años.
2 ¿Vosotros (*estudiar*) en un instituto?
3 Tú (*hablar*) muy bien español.
4 ¿A qué hora (*abrir*) el banco?
5 Lo siento, yo no (*comprender*).
6 Carmen (*recibir*) muchas cartas.

B *Reply to these statements saying that you* **also** *do what is expressed in the sentence. Use* **también** (*also*).

Ejemplo: Peter estudia español.
    Yo también estudio español.
1 Carlos llega a las 9.00.
2 Ellos desayunan a las 8.00.
3 Carmen viaja mucho.
4 Jorge y Miguel beben cerveza.
5 Luisa responde todas sus cartas.
6 Mis primas reciben muchos amigos en casa.

C *Say you don't do what is expressed in the sentence either. Use* **tampoco** (*not . . . either*).
Ejemplo: Antonio no comprende.
    Yo tampoco comprendo.
1 Pedro no responde sus cartas.
2 Mi hermana no escribe mucho.
3 Ellos no beben vino.
4 Ana Luisa no viaja a Sudamérica.
5 Elena no habla alemán.
6 José no desayuna.

D *Answer these questions about yourself.*
1 ¿Vd. trabaja o estudia?
2 ¿Dónde trabaja/estudia?
3 ¿Dónde vive Vd.?
4 ¿Vive Vd. con su familia/con amigos/solo(a)?
5 ¿Qué idiomas habla Vd.? (¿inglés/español/francés/alemán/italiano, etc.?)
6 ¿Viaja Vd. a España?
7 ¿Adónde viaja? (towns)

el idioma *language*

15 Myself, yourself . . .

1 Reflexive verbs

A reflexive verb is one that is normally indicated by -se added to the infinitive, e.g., **levantarse** (*to get up*), **lavarse** (*to wash*). **Se** is sometimes translated into English as *oneself*, e.g., **alegrarse** (*to enjoy oneself*), but often it is not expressed at all. The reflexive pronouns **me, te, se, nos, os, se**, could be said to correspond to forms such as *myself, yourself, himself, herself*, etc.

Reflexive verbs are conjugated in the usual way but with a reflexive pronoun preceding the conjugated verb.

Ejemplo: **levantarse**   *to get up*

me levanto	*I get up*	**nos** levantamos	*we get up*
te levantas	*you get up* (fam.)	**os** levantáis	*you get up*
se levanta	*you get up, he/she gets up*	**se** levantan	*you/they get up*

¿A qué hora **te** levantas?	*What time do you get up?*
Me levanto a las 8.00.	*I get up at 8.00.*
Me lavo y luego desayuno.	*I wash (myself) and then I have breakfast.*

2 Infinitive forms

When there is an infinitive the reflexive pronoun follows the -**ar**, -**er** or -**ir** and becomes one word with the infinitive.

Después de levantar**me** me baño.   *After I get up (or after getting up) I have a bath.*
Antes de acostar**me** leo.   *Before I go to bed (or before going to bed) I read.*

3 Position of the Reflexive Pronoun

In a construction *finite verb* (or conjugated verb) + *infinitive* the reflexive pronoun may either precede the finite verb or be attached to the infinitive (as in number **2** above). The latter is more frequent and probably easier to remember.

Tienes que afeitar**te**.	*You have to shave (yourself).*
Debemos marchar**nos**.	*We must leave.*

But also found, though less frequently:

Te tienes que afeitar.
Nos debemos marchar.

4 List of Reflexive verbs

There is a large number of reflexive verbs in Spanish. Here is a list of some of the most frequent. The **ie**, **ue**, or **i** next to the verb shows that its stem changes in the Present tense. For an explanation of this see Unit 16, pp. 63–5.

acostarse (ue)	*to go to bed*	levantarse	*to get up*
acordarse (ue)	*to remember*	marcharse	*to leave*
afeitarse	*to shave*	morirse (ue)	*to die*
alegrarse	*to enjoy onself*	moverse (ue)	*to move*
bañarse	*to have a bath*	olvidarse	*to forget*
casarse	*to get married*	pararse	*to stop*
cortarse	*to cut oneself*	peinarse	*to comb one's*
despertarse (ie)	*to wake up*		*hair*
equivocarse	*to make a*	probarse (ue)	*to try on*
	mistake	reirse (i)	*to laugh*
hallarse	*to be (situated)*		
herirse (ie)	*to hurt oneself*	sentarse (ie)	*to sit down*
lavarse	*to wash*	sentirse (ie)	*to feel*
		verse	*to meet; to look*

Diálogo: **Tengo que levantarme . . .** (*I must get up . . .*)
A ¿Un café?
B No gracias. Ya es tarde. Debo marcharme. Mañana tengo que levantarme a las 7.00. Además me siento cansada.

debo   *I must, I ought to* (from **deber**)
ya es tarde   *it's already late*
además   *besides*
cansado   *tired*

PRACTIQUE

A   *Add the correct reflexive pronoun:* **me, te, se, nos, os, se.**
1 '¿Cómo . . . sientes (tú)?' — 'Perfectamente, gracias.'
2 (Yo) . . . alegro mucho de estar en España.
3 Raúl y Cristina . . . casan mañana.
4 ¿Por qué . . . marcháis tan pronto?
5 . . . marchamos porque ya es tarde.
6 Karen no habla muy bien español. Siempre . . . equivoca.

tan pronto   *so soon*
siempre   *always*

B   *Complete these sentences with the correct form of the reflexive verb in brackets.*
Ejemplo: Ella (*marcharse*) mañana.
                  Ella se marcha mañana.
1 Julio (*afeitarse*) todos los días.
2 Tú (*levantarse*) siempre muy tarde.
3 Durante las vacaciones yo (*bañarse*) en la piscina.
4 ¿Dónde (*hallarse*) Bilbao?
5 Nosotros no (*olvidarse*) nunca de aquel día.
6 Tu madre (*verse*) muy joven.

durante   *during*
las vacaciones   *holidays*
nunca   *never*

C   *Answer these questions about yourself.*
1 ¿A qué hora se levanta Vd. normalmente?
2 ¿A qué hora se marcha al trabajo/colegio/universidad?
3 ¿A qué hora se acuesta? (Me acuesto . . .)

el trabajo   *work*
el colegio   *school*
la universidad   *university*

16 More about the Present

1 Irregular verbs

There are many verbs in Spanish which do not follow a fixed pattern in their conjugation. They are irregular. Some are irregular only in the first person singular, others in more than one person. Here is a list of verbs which are irregular in the first person singular of the Present tense. Those marked with an asterisk (*) are also stem-changing (see **2** below).

-ar verbs

dar	**doy**	*I give*
estar	**estoy**	*I am*

-er verbs

agradecer	**agradezco**	*I thank*
caer	**caigo**	*I fall*
coger	**cojo**	*I catch, pick up*
conocer	**conozco**	*I know* (a person or place)
hacer	**hago**	*I do, make*
obtener*	**obtengo**	*I obtain*
parecer	**parezco**	*I appear, seem*
pertenecer	**pertenezco**	*I belong*
poner	**pongo**	*I put*
proponer	**propongo**	*I propose*
saber	**sé**	*I know* (a fact)
suponer	**supongo**	*I suppose*
tener*	**tengo**	*I have*
traer	**traigo**	*I bring*
ver	**veo**	*I see*

-ir verbs

conducir	**conduzco**	*I drive*
corregir*	**corrijo**	*I correct*

decir*	**digo**	*I say*
elegir*	**elijo**	*I choose*
oir	**oigo**	*I hear*
salir	**salgo**	*I go out*
venir*	**vengo**	*I come*

Note: **oir** has other changes: **i** changes to **y** in the 2nd and 3rd person singular and the 3rd person plural: **oigo, oyes, oye, oímos, oís, oyen**.

Haber (auxiliary verb *to have*), **ir** (*to go*) and **ser** (*to be*) are irregular and must be learned separately. Here is the first, second and third person singular and the first, second and third person plural of **haber** and **ir**. For **ser** see Unit 3.

haber (*to have*)   *sing.* **he, has, ha**   *pl.* **hemos, habéis, han**

Haber is used to form compound tenses such as the Present perfect shown in the examples below (see Unit 27).

He trabajado.	*I have worked.*
¿**Has** hablado con él?	*Have you spoken to him?*
Hemos terminado.	*We have finished.*

ir (*to go*)   *sing.* **voy, vas, va**   *pl.* **vamos, vais, van**

¿Adónde **vas**?	*Where are you going?*
Voy al cine.	*I'm going to the cinema.*
Vamos al teatro.	*We're going to the theatre.*

Vamos also translates into English as *let's go*.

Diálogo 1: **Salgo a las 9.00** (*I leave at 9.00*)
A   ¿A qué hora sales de casa normalmente?
B   Salgo siempre a las 9.00.
A   ¿Qué haces por la noche?
B   No hago nada en especial. ¿Y tú?
A   Generalmente veo la televisión.

normalmente   *normally*
en especial   *in particular*
generalmente   *usually*

Diálogo 2: ¿Sabe Vd. conducir? (*Do you know how to drive?*)
A ¿Sabe Vd. conducir?
B Sí, sé conducir, pero no conduzco muy bien.
   Siempre conduce mi mujer.

mi mujer *my wife*

PRACTIQUE
A *Change the infinitive into the correct form of the Present tense.*
1 Yo no (*conocer*) muy bien la ciudad porque (*salir*) muy poco.
2 Delia (*ir*) de vacaciones todos los años.
3 Por la tarde yo no (*hacer*) nada.
4 Mi mujer (*salir*) de casa a las 9.30. Yo (*salir*) siempre a las 9.00.
5 Los domingos por la mañana mi mujer y yo (*ir*) a misa.
6 '¿Sabes tú dónde están las llaves?' — 'No, no (*saber*).'

ir de vacaciones *to go on holiday*
ir a misa *to go to mass*
los domingos *Sundays* (for the days of the week see p. 156)

B *Complete these sentences with the appropriate verb from the list:*
conozco, vengo, cojo, traigo, doy, pertenezco.
1 Para ir a la oficina siempre . . . el autobús.
2 Esta noche . . . una fiesta en casa.
3 . . . a José muy bien.
4 . . . a un club de fútbol.
5 . . . aquí todos los días.
6 . . . algo para Vd.

esta noche *tonight*

2 Stem-changing verbs

Some verbs undergo a change in the stem (the main part of the verb
without its ending) which occurs only when the stem is stressed.
Therefore, the first and second person plural are not affected by this
change. Stem-changing verbs have the same endings as regular verbs.
Here is a list of the most common stem-changing verbs in the Present
tense.

64   *More about the Present*

(*a*)   Verbs which change **e** to **ie**:

-**ar**:		-**er**:	
cerrar	*to close, shut*	encender	*to light, turn on*
despertar(se)	*to wake up*	entender	*to understand*
empezar	*to begin*	perder	*to lose*
nevar	*to snow*	querer	*to want*
pensar	*to think*	tener	*to have*

-**ir**:			
herirse	*to hurt oneself*	sentir(se)	*to feel*
preferir	*to prefer*	venir	*to come*

Here is an example of one of the above verbs in all its forms:

> **entender**   *to understand*
> entiendo   *I understand*
> entiendes   *you understand* (fam.)
> entiende   *you understand, he/she understands*
> entendemos   *we understand*
> entendéis   *you understand* (fam.)
> entienden   *you/they understand*

(*b*)   Verbs which change **o** to **ue**:

-**ar**:		-**er**:	
acostarse	*to go to bed*	devolver	*to return, give bac*
acordarse	*to remember*	doler	*to hurt, feel pain*
comprobar	*to check*	llover	*to rain*
contar	*to tell, count*	moverse	*to move*
encontrar	*to find*	poder	*to be able*
mostrar	*to show*	soler	*to be accustomed*
recordar	*to remember*	volver	*to return*
rogar	*to ask, beg*		

-**ir**:	
dormir(se)	*to sleep, go to sle*
morir(se)	*to die*

Note: **jugar**, whose stem has a **u**, also changes into **ue**: **jue**go, **jue**gas, **jue**ga, etc.

Here is an example of one of the above verbs in all its forms:

volver   *to return*
vuelvo   *I return*
vuelves   *you return* (fam.)
vuelve   *you return, he/she returns*
volvemos   *we return*
volvéis   *you return* (fam.)
vuelven   *you/they return*

(*c*)   Verbs which change **e** to **i**:

conseguir	*to get*	reir(se)	*to laugh*
corregir	*to correct*	repetir	*to repeat*
elegir	*to choose*	seguir	*to follow, continue*
pedir	*to ask (for)*	servir	*to serve*

Notice also the change in the 1st person singular of:

conseguir – consigo; **corregir** – corrijo; **elegir** – elijo; **seguir** – sigo.

servir   *to serve*
sirvo   *I serve*
sirves   *you serve* (fam.)
sirve   *you serve, he/she serves*
servimos   *we serve*
servís   *you serve* (fam.)
sirven   *you/they serve*

Diálogo 3: ¿Vienes al partido? (*Are you coming to the match?*)
A   ¿Vienes al partido esta tarde?
B   Sí, ¿a qué hora empieza?
A   A las 5.00.
B   ¿Tienes entradas?
A   Sí, tengo una.
B   ¿Cuánto cuestan?
A   Mil pesetas.

las entradas   *tickets*

Diálogo 4: ¿Prefiere blanco o tinto? (*Do you prefer white or red?*)
A   Buenas tardes. Quiero una botella de vino, por favor.
B   ¿Prefiere blanco o tinto?
A   Prefiero tinto.

    B ¿Quiere algo más?
    A Nada más, gracias.

una botella de vino   *a bottle of wine*

PRACTIQUE
C *Transform the infinitive into the correct form of the Present tense.*
1 ¿Vd. (*entender*) bien el español?
2 Yo no (*entender*) nada.
3 ¿A qué hora (*empezar*) la película?
4 Andrés (*venir*) mañana.
5 Yo no (*recordar*) nada.
6 ¿Cuándo (*volver*) tus padres?

la película   *film*

D *Answer these questions about yourself. Use complete sentences in your reply.*
1 ¿Conoce Vd. España?
2 ¿Qué países conoce Vd.?
3 ¿Entiende Vd. el español/el francés?
4 ¿Va Vd. al extranjero (*abroad*) en sus vacaciones?
5 ¿Juega Vd. al tenis/fútbol, etc.?

17 Passive and impersonal expressions

1 Passive voice

Look at these sentences in English.

> Many people *speak* Spanish.
> Spanish *is spoken* by many people.

The first is an active sentence with an active verb: 'Many people speak Spanish'. The second is passive: 'Spanish is spoken (by many people)'. In the passive sentence 'Spanish' is the subject and 'many people' is the agent, who carries out the action expressed by the verb. In Spanish there are also active and passive sentences:

> Mucha gente **habla** español. (Active)
> El español **es hablado** por mucha gente. (Passive)

(a) *Ser* + **past participle**

There are two main ways of forming passive sentences in Spanish. As in the sentence above we may use the verb **ser** plus a past participle. The past participle is formed by adding the ending **-ado** to the stem of **-ar** verbs and **-ido** to the stem of **-er** and **-ir** verbs. For example:

(hablar)	**Es** habl**ado**	*It's spoken.*
(vender)	**Es** vend**ido**	*It's sold.*
(conducir)	**Es** conduc**ido**	*It's driven.*

In this context the past participle will change for gender and number.

> El español es hablad**o** por mucha gente.   *Spanish is spoken by many people.*
> Esta lengua es hablad**a** por mucha gente.   *This language is spoken by many people.*
> El inglés y el español son hablad**os** por mucha gente.   *English and Spanish are spoken by many people.*

For a list of irregular past participles see Unit 21, p. 84.

(*b*)   *Se* + **3rd person of the verb**

The passive construction with **ser** + past participle, although not so frequent in Spanish, is normally used when the agent is expressed, e.g., **por mucha gente**. If the agent is not stated we may use another passive construction with the word **se** plus a verb in the third person.

> El español **se habla** en muchos países.   *Spanish is spoken in many countries.*
> Aquí **se habla** español.   *Spanish is spoken here.*

In this type of sentence the verb must agree with the subject in number.

> Este coche **se vende** en España.   *This car is sold in Spain.*
> Estos coches **se venden** en España.   *These cars are sold in Spain.*

In the previous sentences **hablar** and **vender** are not reflexive verbs but normal verbs, although we use the **se** of reflexive verbs (see Unit 15, p. 58).

> *Diálogo 1:* **Se venden en Correos** (*They're sold at the post-office*)
> *A*   ¿Tiene sellos (*stamps*)?
> *B*   No, aquí no vendemos sellos. Los sellos se venden en Correos.
> *A*   Gracias.

> *Diálogo 2:* ¿**Qué idioma se habla?** (*What language is spoken?*)
> *A*   ¿Qué idioma se habla en México?
> *B*   Se habla español.
> *A*   ¿Y en Argentina?
> *B*   Allí también se habla español.

PRACTIQUE

A   *Transform these sentences as in the example.*
Ejemplo: Los españoles beben mucho café.   (España)
            En España se bebe mucho café.
1   Los ingleses **beben** mucho té.   (Inglaterra)
2   Los andaluces **comen** mucho pescado.   (Andalucía)
3   Los chilenos **hablan** español.   (Chile)

4 Los españoles **dan** mucha importancia a las fiestas.   (España)
5 Los brasileños **hablan** portugués.   (Brasil)
6 Los ingleses **conducen** por la izquierda.   (Inglaterra)

el té   *tea*
el pescado   *fish*
por la izquierda   *on (along) the left*

B   *Make up passive sentences using the words given below.*
Ejemplo: Las medicinas – vender – la farmacia.
            Las medicinas se venden en la farmacia.
1 El pan – comprar – la panadería.
2 La fruta y las verduras – vender – el mercado.
3 La gasolina – vender – la estación de servicio.
4 Los cheques de viajero – cambiar – el banco.
5 Las cartas – echar – Correos.
6 Los seguros – obtener – la agencia de viajes.

los cheques de viajero   *traveller's cheques*
cambiar   *to change*
echar una carta   *to post a letter*
obtener un seguro   *to get insurance*
la agencia de viajes   *travel agency*

2   Impersonal sentences

Se is also used to form impersonal sentences, in which case it
translates into English as *one, they, you* or *people*.

> ¿Por dónde **se va** a Granada?   *How does one get to Granada?*
> **Se sale** del hotel a las 8.00.   *You leave (or one leaves) the hotel
> at 8.00.*
> **Se llega** a las 12.00.   *You arrive (or one arrives) at 12.00.*
> **Se dice** que es interesante.   *It is said (or they/people say) it is
> interesting.*

Here are some useful sentences with **se**:

> ¿Cómo se dice esto en español?   *How does one say this in
> Spanish?*

¿Cómo se escribe (su nombre/apellido)? *How do you spell (your name/surname)?*
¿Cómo se pronuncia esta palabra? *How do you pronounce this word?*

As in English, we can also form impersonal sentences with the third person plural of the verb.

Dicen que es diferente. *They say it is different.*
Allí **hablan** español. *They speak Spanish there.*

Diálogo 3: ¿**Por dónde se va** . . . ? (*How does one get to . . . ?*)
A Perdone, ¿por dónde se va a Zaragoza?
B Se puede ir por la autopista o por la carretera nacional.
A ¿Y en tren se tarda mucho?
B Pues, se tarda tres horas más o menos.

la autopista *motorway*
la carretera nacional *A or arterial road*
tardar *to take time*
pues . . . *well* . . .

PRACTIQUE
C *Make up impersonal sentences with* **se**.
Ejemplo: Dicen que es importante.
           Se dice que es importante.
1 Piensan que es posible.
2 Creen que está en Marbella.
3 ¿A qué hora salimos de Madrid?
4 ¿A qué hora llegamos a Toledo?
5 ¿Qué carretera tomamos para ir a Avila?
6 ¿Dónde cogemos el autobús?

importante *important*
posible *possible*

18   Using verbal combinations

Verb + infinitive

As in English, a number of Spanish verbs can be combined with infinitives to express a variety of ideas. Here is a list of the most important.

ir a	*to be going to*	
tener que	*to have to*	
querer	*to want to*	+ infinitive
preferir	*to prefer to*	
poder	*to be able to*	
deber	*to have to, ought to*	

¿Qué **vas a** hacer?	*What are you going to do?*
Voy a trabajar.	*I'm going to work.*
¿Qué **tienes que** hacer?	*What have you got to do?*
No tengo nada que hacer.	*I have nothing to do.*
¿Qué **quieres** comer?	*What do you want to eat?*
Quiero comer un bocadillo.	*I want to eat a sandwich.*
¿**Puedes** venir la próxima semana?	*Can you come next week?*
No puedo venir.	*I cannot come.*
¿Qué **debo** hacer?	*What must I do?*
Vd. **debe** volver el próximo lunes.	*You must come back next Monday.*

Deber is a regular verb. For the conjugation of the other verbs see Unit 8 (**tener**), and Unit 16 (**ir, querer, preferir, poder**).

1   Verbs requiring *a* before infinitive

Certain verbs require the preposition **a** before an infinitive.

aprender a	*to learn to*	invitar a	*to invite to*
ayudar a	*to help to*	ir a	*to go to, to go and*
empezar a	*to begin to*	llegar a	*to come to, to succeed*
enseñar a	*to teach to*	venir a	*to come to, to come and*

Empieza a llover. *It starts to rain.*
Voy a buscar a Juan. *I'm going to fetch Juan.*
Venimos a descansar. *We come (here) to rest.*

2 Verbs requiring *de* before infinitive

Other verbs take **de** before an infinitive.

acabar de	*to stop, to have just*	dejar de	*to stop, to fail*
acordarse de	*to remember to (about)*	no dejar de	*to be sure to, not to fail to*
alegrarse de	*to be glad to*	olvidarse de	*to forget to*
cansarse de	*to tire of*		

Elena **acaba** de llegar. *Elena has just arrived.*
¿**Se acuerda** Vd. de Raúl? *Do you remember Raúl?*
Me alegro de estar aquí. *I'm glad to be here.*
Siempre **me olvido** de cerrar *I always forget to close the*
   la puerta.   *door.*

3 Infinitive to replace present participle

Generally in Spanish, after a preposition we use an infinitive while in English we would use a present participle (*before arriving, after reading, without thinking*). Here is a list of some important prepositions used with infinitives.

antes de (entrar)	*before (entering)*
después de (salir)	*after (going out)*
para (hablar)	*in order to (speak)*
sin (parar)	*without (stopping)*
al (llegar)	*on (arriving)*

Al + infinitive is a very frequent construction in Spanish. Here are some further examples:

Siempre saluda **al entrar**.   *He always says hello when he comes in (on entering).*

Al terminar bebe un café.   *When he finishes (on finishing) he drinks some coffee.*

Diálogo 1: Quiero llamar por teléfono (*I want to make a telephone call*)

A   Perdone. Quiero llamar por teléfono. ¿Puedo llamar desde aquí?

B   ¿Al extranjero o dentro de España?

A   Al extranjero.

B   Lo siento, en ese caso tiene que ir a la Telefónica. Está muy cerca de aquí.

al extranjero   *abroad*

Diálogo 2: Acaba de salir (*He has just gone out*)

A   Buenas tardes. Vengo a ver al señor Martínez.

B   Lo siento, pero el señor Martínez acaba de salir. ¿Quiere dejar algún recado?

A   No, prefiero volver más tarde.

dejar un recado   *to leave a message*
más tarde   *later*

PRACTIQUE

A   *Answer each of these questions with the phrase* **voy a** + *infinitive.*
Ejemplo: ¿Qué vas a hacer? (salir)
          Voy a salir.

1 ¿Qué vas a comprar? (una camisa)
2 ¿Dónde vas a cenar? (en casa)
3 ¿A qué hora vas a volver? (a las 8.00)
4 ¿Cuándo vas a viajar? (en octubre)
5 ¿Qué vas a hacer? (nada)
6 ¿Cuál vas a escoger? (el negro)

B   *Complete the sentences below with a Spanish expression.*
Ejemplo: (*We are glad to*) estar en Barcelona.
        Nos alegramos de estar en Barcelona.

1 (*I have to*) estar allí a las 6.00.
2 (*They want to*) pasar las vacaciones en Marbella.
3 (*He prefers to*) viajar en avión.
4 (*They can't*) salir esta tarde.
5 (*She has just*) volver de Londres.
6 (*I must*) levantarme a las 7.00.

19 Saying (to) me, (to) him . . .

1 Direct object pronouns

Look at this sentence:

> Yo alquilo el coche.   *I hire the car.*

Here the subject of the sentence is **yo**, the verb is **alquilo** (from **alquilar**, *to hire, rent*). Now observe these two sentences:

> Yo alquilo el coche.   *I hire the car.*
> **Lo** alquilo.   *I hire it.*

In order to avoid repetition of the noun **el coche**, we have used **lo**. **Lo** is a direct object pronoun. Here it refers back to the object **el coche**.
  Object pronouns can be masculine or feminine, singular or plural.

> Cristina reserva la habitación.   *Cristina books the room.*
> Cristina **la** reserva.   *Cristina books it.*
> José compra las entradas.   *José buys the tickets.*
> José **las** compra.   *José buys them.*
> Miro los libros.   *I look at the books.*
> **Los** miro.   *I look at them.*

Direct object pronouns can also refer to people. Look at these sentences:

> ¿Conoces **a** Carmen?   *Do you know Carmen?*
> ¿Vas a invitar **a** Javier?   *Are you going to invite Javier?*

Carmen and Javier are here direct objects. A peculiarity of Spanish is that the preposition **a** is placed before a direct object if the object is a definite person. This use of the preposition **a** is known as 'personal **a**'. In both sentences the direct object can be substituted by a pronoun.

> ¿**La** conoces?   *Do you know her?*
> ¿**Le** conoces?   *Do you know him?*
> ¿**Les** conoces?   *Do you know them?*

Le and **les** are masculine forms (**les** also stands for masculine and feminine together). However, in certain regions of Spain and in Latin America you will hear **lo** and **los** used for people. Both usages are correct. The following rule may be easier to remember when using the masculine form of direct object pronouns:

> Use **lo** and **los** for things.
> Use **le** and **les** for people.

In direct address, **le** and **la** and **les** and **las** also stand for **usted** and **ustedes**, respectively:

> Yo **le** invito.   *I invite you* (masc.)
> Yo **la** invito.   *I invite you* (fem.)
> Yo **les/las** invito.   *I invite you* (masc./fem., pl.)

Here is a table of the direct object pronouns for the third person singular and third person plural.

sing.	masc.	**le**	*you/him*
	masc.	**lo**	*it* (also *you/him*)
	fem.	**la**	*you/her/it*
pl.	masc.	**les**	*you/them* (people)
	masc.	**los**	*you/them* (people and things)
	fem.	**las**	*you/them* (people and things)

Other object pronouns are:

me	*me*	Ella **me** quiere.	*She loves me.*
te	*you* (fam., sing.)	**Te** quiero.	*I love you*
nos	*us*	El **nos** invita.	*He invites us.*
os	*you* (fam., pl.)	**Os** invito.	*I invite you.*

Position of direct object pronouns

The normal position of the object pronoun is before the finite (or conjugated) verb, as shown in the examples above. However, in phrases where a finite verb precedes an infinitive, the object pronoun may either precede thè finite verb or be attached to the infinitive:

> Quiero hacer**lo**.   *I want to do it.*
> **Lo** quiero hacer.   *I want to do it.*

Voy a invitar**la**.	*I'm going to invite her.*
La voy a invitar.	*I'm going to invite her.*

***Diálogo 1:* Le conozco muy bien** (*I know him very well*)

A ¿Conoces a Alfonso?

B Sí, le conozco muy bien.

A Vive cerca de tu casa, ¿verdad?

B Sí, sí. Le veo casi todos los días.

casi *almost*

***Diálogo 2:* ¿Me oye Vd.?** (*Do you hear me?*)

A (*En el teléfono*) ¿Sí?

B Buenas tardes. ¿Está Patricia?

A Perdone, pero no le oigo bien.

B Quiero hablar con Patricia, por favor.
¿Me oye usted ahora?

A Sí, ahora le oigo perfectamente.

PRACTIQUE

A *Complete these sentences with the correct object pronoun.*

1 '¿Conoces a Luis y Juan?' – 'No, no . . . conozco.'
2 '¿Ves mucho a María?' – 'Sí, . . . veo todos los días.'
3 '¿Ves aquel libro?' – 'No, no . . . veo. ¿Dónde está?'
4 '¿Escuchas la radio?' – 'Sí, . . . escucho siempre.'
5 '¿Visitas mucho a tus padres?' – ' . . . visito muy poco.'
6 '¿Ves mucho la televisión?' – '. . . veo todas las noches.'

2 Indirect object pronouns

Look at this sentence:

Ahora (yo) le doy la cuenta. *I'll give you the bill now.*

Here, the subject of the sentence is **yo**, the verb is **doy** (*I give*, from **dar**, *to give*), the direct object is **la cuenta** (the thing given) and the indirect object is **le** (**a usted**, *to you*, that is, the person to whom **la cuenta** is given).

Indirect object pronouns can be singular or plural.

> **Le** doy la cuenta (a usted, a él, a ella). *I give you* (sing.) */him/her the bill.*
> **Les** doy la cuenta (a ustedes, a ellos). *I give you* (pl.)/*them the bill.*

With indirect object pronouns there is no distinction between masculine and feminine. **Le** stands for **a él** (*to him*), **a ella** (*to her*) and **a usted** (*to you*, sing.). **Les** stands for **a ellos** (*to them*, masc.), **a ellas** (*to them*, fem.) and **a ustedes** (*to you*, pl.).

To avoid ambiguity **a él, a ella, a usted** or an actual noun can be added after the verb, but still keeping the indirect object pronoun **le**.

> **Le** doy la cuenta **a él**. *I give the bill to him.*
> **Le** doy la cuenta **al señor**. *I give the bill to the gentleman.*

Likewise **a ellos, a ellas, a ustedes** or an actual noun can be used after the verb in a construction with **les**.

> **Les** escribo una carta **a ellas**. *I write a letter to them.*
> **Les** escribo **a mis padres**. *I write to my parents.*

The use of two indirect objects referring to the same person (as above) is a common feature of colloquial Spanish.

Sometimes the indirect object may be a thing, in which case **le** or **les** must be used:

> No **le** pongo azúcar al té. *I don't put sugar in tea.*
> ¿**Le** pongo más sal? *Shall I put more salt in it?*

Other indirect object pronouns are similar to direct object pronouns:

> ¿**Me** da la cuenta? *Will you give me the bill?*
> ¿**Te** doy el dinero? *Shall I give you the money?*
> ¿**Nos** trae la carta? *Will you bring us the menu?*
> **Os** digo la verdad. *I'm telling you the truth.*

Here is a table of the indirect object pronouns.

me	*to me*
te	*to you* (fam.)
le	*to you/him/her/it*

nos	*to us*
os	*to you* (fam.)
les	*to you/them*

Position of indirect object pronouns

The position of indirect object pronouns is the same as that of direct object pronouns, that is, normally before the verb. But when there are two object pronouns in a sentence, one indirect and one direct, the indirect object must come first.

| El camarero **me** da la cuenta. | *The waiter gives me the bill.* |
| El camarero **me la** da. | *The waiter gives it to me.* |

When the indirect object **le** or **les** precedes **lo, la, los** or **las**, the indirect object becomes **se**.

El camarero **le** da la cuenta.	*The waiter gives him the bill.*
El camarero **se** la da.	*The waiter gives it to him.*
¿**Le** digo la verdad?	*Shall I tell you the truth?*
¿**Se** la digo?	*Shall I tell it to you?*

Diálogo 3: **Ahora se la doy** (*I'll give it to you now*)
A ¿La llave de la habitación 30, por favor?
B Sí, un momentito. Ahora se la doy.
A Gracias.

un momentito *diminutive from* **un momento**

Diálogo 4: ¿**Puede traérmelo . . .** ? (*Can you bring it to me . . . ?*)
A ¿A qué hora le traigo el desayuno?
B ¿Puede traérmelo a las 8.30?
A Sí, cómo no. ¿Le traigo café o té?
B Prefiero café. Y un zumo de naranja también, por favor.
A Entonces tenemos un café con leche y un zumo de naranja.
B Eso es. Muchísimas gracias.

cómo no *certainly*	**entonces** *then*
un zumo *juice*	**eso es** *that's right*
	muchísimas gracias *many thanks*

PRACTIQUE

B   *Reply to each of these requests saying you will do what is asked straight away. Follow the example.*

Ejemplo: Me da su pasaporte, por favor.
             Ahora se lo doy.

1 Me da la llave de la habitación, por favor.
2 Me dice su número de teléfono, por favor.
3 Me pasa la mantequilla, por favor.
4 Me pasa el pan, por favor.
5 Me cambia estas 5.000 pesetas, por favor.
6 Me da su dirección, por favor.

la mantequilla   *butter*

20 Saying what you are doing

1 Present participle

To say what you or someone else is doing we use either the Present
tense or the verb **estar** followed by a present participle or gerund.

¿Qué haces?	*What are you doing?*
¿Qué **estás haciendo**?	*What are you doing?*
Llamo a mi novia.	*I'm calling my girlfriend.*
Estoy llamando a mi novia.	*I'm calling my girlfriend.*

2 Endings of the present participle

(*a*) The present participle forms are equivalent to the English *-ing*
forms (*writing, working*). In Spanish there are two endings: -**ar** verbs
form the present participle or gerund with -**ando**.

Estoy trabaj**ando**.	*I'm working.*
Estamos estudi**ando**.	*We're studying.*

-**er** and -**ir** verbs form the present participle with -**iendo**.

Julio está escrib**iendo**.	*Julio is writing.*
Mercedes está com**iendo**.	*Mercedes is eating.*

(*b*) Verbs ending in -**ir** which change the stem from **e** to **i** (see Unit
16, pp. 64–5) also show this change·in the present participle.

pedir	pido	pidiendo
repetir	repito	repitiendo

Verbs which change **e** into **ie** also take **i** in the present participle. This
does not apply to -**ar** and -**er** verbs.

preferir	prefiero	prefiriendo
sentirse	me siento	sintiéndose

-ir and certain **-er** verbs which change **o** into **ue** take **u** in the present participle.

dormir	duermo	durmiendo	(*sleeping*)
morir	muero	muriendo	(*dying*)
poder	puedo	pudiendo	(*being able to*)

The present participle of **ir** is **yendo** (*going*) and of **leer** is **leyendo** (*reading*).

3 Position of pronoun with present participle

When the phrase contains a pronoun, this may go before the verb **estar** or it may be added to the end of the present participle, in which case the word must carry an accent.

Lo estoy usando.	*I'm using it.*
Estoy usándo**lo**.	*I'm using it.*
Lo estoy escribiendo.	*I'm writing it.*
Estoy escribiéndo**lo**.	*I'm writing it.*

4 Expressions using the present participle

The present participle is also used with the verbs **ir, venir, andar, seguir** and **continuar**.

Esto va cambiando poco a poco.   *This is changing little by little.*
Viene ocurriendo desde 1985.   *It's been happening since 1985.*
¿Qué andas buscando?   *What are you looking for?*
Sigue lloviendo.   *It continues raining/It's still raining.*
Continúo trabajando allí.   *I continue working there/I'm still working there.*

5 Use of infinitive

The English gerund is not always equivalent to the Spanish present participle. In fact, Spanish often uses an infinitive where English uses a gerund, for example, after prepositions (see also Unit 18, p. 72).

Without thinking.	Sin pensar.
Before arriving.	Antes de llegar.
Smoking is prohibited.	Se prohibe fumar.

***Diálogo 1:* ¿Qué estás haciendo?** (*What are you doing?*)

A ¿Qué estás haciendo?

B Estoy preparando la cena.

¿Quieres cenar con nosotros?

B Gracias, pero estoy trabajando.

preparar *to prepare*

***Diálogo 2:* Está lloviendo** (*It's raining*)

A ¿Qué tal el tiempo?

B Está lloviendo.

A ¡Hombre! ¡Qué lástima!

¿Qué tal . . . ? *How is . . . ?*

¡Hombre! is a frequent interjection in Spanish. In this context it could be translated as '*Oh really!*'

PRACTIQUE

A *Say what you and other people are doing.*

Ejemplo: ¿Qué estás haciendo? (trabajo)

Estoy trabajando.

1 ¿Qué está haciendo Eduardo? (desayuna)

2 ¿Qué estáis haciendo vosotros? (estudiamos)

3 ¿Qué están haciendo los niños? (juegan)

4 ¿Qué estás haciendo? (leo)

5 ¿Qué están haciendo ustedes? (comemos)

6 ¿Qué está haciendo usted? (tomo el sol)

B *Answer these questions saying you are doing what is being asked.*

Ejemplo: ¿Vas a preparar la cena?

Estoy preparándola.

1 ¿Vas a escribir la carta?

2 ¿Vas a escribirles a tus hermanos?

3 ¿Vas a responderle a tu padre?

4 ¿Vas a lavar la ropa?

5 ¿Vas a limpiar el piso?

6 ¿Vas a servir la comida?

lavar *to wash*
la ropa *clothes*
limpiar *to clean*

21 Saying what is done

1 *Estar* + past participle

To express the result or outcome of an event, for example *it is finished*, *it is booked*, we may use the verb **estar** followed by a past participle. To form the past participle we add **-ado** to the stem of **-ar** verbs and **-ido** to the stem of **-er** and **-ir** verbs (see also Unit 17, p. 67).

In this context the past participle must agree in gender and number with the noun it describes.

> La cena está termin**ada**.   *Dinner is finished.*
> Las habitaciones están reser**vadas**.   *The rooms are booked.*
> Estoy cans**ado**.   *I'm tired.*

2 Irregular past participles

Some verbs form the past participle in an irregular way. Here is a list of the most frequent irregular past participles:

abrir (*to open*)   **abierto**
decir (*to say*)   **dicho**
despertar (*to wake up*)   **despierto**
devolver (*to give back*)   **devuelto**
envolver (*to wrap up*)   **envuelto**
escribir (*to write*)   **escrito**
hacer (*to do, make*)   **hecho**
morir (*to die*)   **muerto**
poner (*to put*)   **puesto**
romper (*to break*)   **roto**
ver (*to see*)   **visto**
volver (*to return, come back*)   **vuelto**

> El banco está abierto.   *The bank is open.*
> Estoy despierto.   *I'm awake.*

El paquete está envuelto. *The packet is wrapped.*
Las cartas están escritas. *The letters are written.*
Las camas están hechas. *The beds are made.*
Mis abuelos están muertos. *My grandparents are dead.*
La mesa está puesta. *The table is laid.*
El vaso está roto. *The glass is broken.*

Diálogo 1: Está abierto (*It's open*)
A Perdone, ¿a qué hora abre el banco?
B Ya está abierto.
A ¿Y hasta qué hora está abierto?
B Hasta las dos de la tarde.

Diálogo 2: Ya está puesta (*It's already laid*)
A ¡Hola! ¿Está hecha la comida?
B Sí, está lista.
A ¿Pongo la mesa?
B Ya está puesta.

estar listo *to be ready*
poner la mesa *to lay the table*

PRACTIQUE
Complete these sentences with **estar** + *past participle.*
Ejemplo: El museo (*cerrar*).
          El museo está cerrado.
1 La farmacia (*abrir*).
2 Estos platos (*romper*).
3 Todo (*decir*).
4 Las reservas (*hacer*).
5 El problema (*terminar*).
6 El examen (*corregir*).

22   Expressing likes and opinions

1   *Gustar*

To say whether we like or dislike something we can use the verb
gustar. It is a special kind of verb which is normally used in the third
person singular or plural, depending on the number of the noun
which follows. The verb must be preceded by an indirect object
pronoun. Here is **gustar** in the Present tense.

me gusta(n)		*I like*	
te gusta(n)	la(s)	*you like* (fam.)	*the*
le gusta(n)	playa(s)	*you like*	*beach(es)*
le gusta(n)		*he/she likes*	
nos gusta(n)		*we like*	
os gusta(n)		*you like* (fam.)	
les gusta(n)	el (los)	*you like*	*the*
les gusta(n)	lago(s)	*they like*	*lake(s)*

¿Le gusta la playa?	*Do you like the beach?*
Sí, me gusta mucho.	*Yes, I like it very much.*
¿Te gustan los lagos?	*Do you like lakes?*
Me gustan.	*I like them.*
¿Os gusta este lugar?	*Do you like this place?*
No nos gusta.	*We don't like it.*

2   *Gustar* + infinitive

Gustar may also be used with a verb (the infinitive) to say whether
you like or dislike doing something. Here **gustar** must go in the third
person singular.

Me gusta nadar.	*I like swimming.*
No les gusta bailar.	*They don't like dancing.*
¿Te gusta pintar?	*Do you like painting?*

Note: if you want to specify *who* likes or dislikes something you have to use the word **a** before the name of the person.

A Gustavo le gusta el tenis.	*Gustavo likes tennis.*
A Clara le gusta correr.	*Clara likes running.*

3 *A mí me gusta*

If you want to be emphatic or wish to establish a contrast, you must use another set of pronouns before the construction with *gustar*.

a mí	me gusta(n)	*I like it (them)*
a ti	te gusta(n)	*you like it (them)*
a usted	le gusta(n)	*you like it (them)*
a él/ella	le gusta(n)	*he/she likes it (them)*
a nosotros	nos gusta(n)	*we like it (them)*
a vosotros	os gusta(n)	*you like it (them)*
a ustedes	les gusta(n)	*you like it (them)*
a ellos/ellas	les gusta(n)	*they like it (them)*

> A mí me gusta mucho el fútbol. ¿Y a usted? *I like football very much. Do you (like it)?*
>
> | A mí no me gusta. | *I don't like it.* |
> |---|---|
> | A mí tampoco. | *Neither do I.* |

This new set of pronouns also helps to clarify the meaning of **le** and **les**. Compare:

Le gusta.	*You like it, he/she likes it.*
A usted le gusta.	*You like it.*
A él le gusta.	*He likes it.*
A ella le gusta.	*She likes it.*

Mí, ti, usted, ella, etc. are also generally used after prepositions: e.g. **para mí** (*for me*), **sin ti** (*without you*).

88 *Expressing likes and opinions*

Note: For a comprehensive study of prepositions refer to Unit 37.

Diálogo 1: No me gustan nada (*I don't like them at all*)
A ¿Qué te gusta hacer en tu tiempo libre?
B Me gusta pasear. ¿Y a ti?
A A mí me gusta hacer deportes.
B ¿Qué deporte te gusta?
A Me gusta el tenis.
B ¿Te gustan los toros?
A No, no me gustan nada.

el tiempo libre *spare time*   **hacer deportes** *to practise sports*
pasear *to go for a walk*   **los toros** *bull-fighting* (*also bulls*)

PRACTIQUE

A *Say you like or dislike each of the following using* **me gusta(n)** *or* **no me gusta(n)**.
Ejemplo: Los deportes (*sports*).
        (No) me gustan los deportes.
1 El verano (*summer*).   4 El otoño (*autumn*).
2 El invierno (*winter*).   5 Las flores (*flowers*).
3 La primavera (*spring*).   6 Las Navidades (*Christmas*).

B *Ask questions with* **gustar** *using the familiar pronoun* **te**.
Ejemplo: Esta escuela (*this school*).
        ¿Te gusta esta escuela?
1 El curso (*course*).
2 Los profesores (*teachers*).
3 La universidad (*university*).
4 Los estudiantes (*students*).
5 Aprender español (*learning Spanish*).
6 Enseñar (*teaching*).

4 Expressing an opinion

To express an opinion you may use the verb **parecer**, an **-er** verb, which follows the same pattern as **gustar: me, te, le, nos, os, les parece/parecen**.

Me parece bonito.	*It seems nice to me.*
	(or *I think it's nice*)
¿Qué te parece?	*What do you think?*
Nos parecen bien.	*They seem all right to us.*
	(or *We think they are all right*)

Diálogo 2: ¿**Qué te parece Madrid?** (*What do you think of Madrid?*)

A ¿Qué te parece Madrid?
B Me parece interesante.
A ¿Y qué te parecen los españoles?
B Me gustan mucho. Me parecen muy simpáticos.
A A mí también.

PRACTIQUE

C *Give your opinion using* **me parece** *or* **me parecen**, *as appropriate.*
Ejemplo: El hotel — barato.
El hotel me parece barato.

1 El tiempo — estupendo.
2 Las playas — excelentes.
3 La comida — muy buena.
4 Los camareros — agradables.
5 La habitación — muy calurosa.
6 El servicio — regular.

Note: opinions may also be given with the verbs **creer** (*to think, believe*), **pensar** (*to think, believe*), **considerar** (*to consider*), using the appropriate ending for each person.

Creo que es fácil.	*I think (that) it's easy.*
Pienso que es malo.	*I think (that) it's bad.*
Lo considero extraño.	*I consider it strange.*
¿Qué piensa Vd.?	*What do you think?*

5 Some more verbs of feeling

Here is a list of verbs not always directly related to likes and opinions which follow the same pattern as **gustar** and **parecer**.

90   *Expressing likes and opinions*

(a) **doler** (*to hurt*) (o > ue)
Me duele la cabeza/el estómago.   *I have a headache/stomach-ache.*
Me duelen los pies.   *My feet ache.*

(b) **importar** (*to mind*)
¿Le importa si fumo?   *Do you mind if I smoke?*
No me importa.   *I don't mind.*

(c) **interesar** (*to interest*)
No me interesa.   *It doesn't interest me.*
¿Te interesa esto?   *Does this interest you?*

(d) **molestar** (*to bother*)
¿Le molesta si abro la ventana?   *Does it bother you if I open the window?*
A mí no me molesta en absoluto.   *I don't mind at all.*

(e) **pasar** (*to happen*)
¿Qué te pasa?   *What's the matter with you?*
No me pasa nada.   *There's nothing wrong with me.*

(f) **sorprender** (*to be surprised*)
Me sorprende.   *It surprises me.*
No nos sorprende.   *It doesn't surprise us.*

23 Talking about past events

1 Preterite tense

Spanish, like English, has several ways of talking about past events. The most useful tense in this context is the Preterite which corresponds to the English Simple Past tense (*I got up, I went out*). There are two sets of endings for this tense: one for **-ar** verbs and another one for verbs in **-er** and **-ir**. Here is the Preterite tense of a regular **-ar** verb.

pasar (*to spend time*)

pas**é**		*I spent*	
pas**aste**		*you spent* (fam.)	
pas**ó**	un año	*you/he/she spent*	a year
pas**amos**	allí	*we spent*	there
pas**asteis**		*you spent* (fam.)	
pas**aron**		*you/they spent*	

Note that the first person plural, **pasamos**, is the same as for the Present tense.

> ¿Dónde pasaste tus vacaciones? *Where did you spend your holidays?*
> Las pasé en Marbella. *I spent them in Marbella.*

These are the endings of regular **-er** and **-ir** verbs.

nacer (*to be born*)

nac**í**		*I was born*	
nac**iste**		*you were born* (fam.)	
nac**ió**		*you were, he/she was born*	
nac**imos**	en España	*we were born*	in Spain
nac**isteis**		*you were born* (fam.)	
nac**ieron**		*you/they were born*	

¿Cuándo nació Vd. (naciste tú)?   *Where were you born?*
Nací el 25 de abril de 1958.   *I was born on the 25th April 1958*
¿Dónde nació Vd. (naciste tú)?   *Where were you born?*
Nací en España.   *I was born in Spain.*

salir (*to leave, to go out*)

salí		I left	
saliste		you left (fam.)	
salió		you/he/she left	
salimos	el martes	we left	on Tuesday
salisteis		you left (fam.)	
salieron		you/they left	

Note that the first person plural, **salimos**, is the same as for the Present tense.

¿En qué fecha salieron de Algeciras?   *On what date did they leave Algeciras?*
Salimos de Los Angeles el sábado 4 de septiembre.   *We left Los Angeles on Saturday 4th of September.*
El avión salió a tiempo.   *The plane left on time.*

Diálogo 1: ¿Dónde lo aprendiste? (*Where did you learn it?*)
A   Hablas muy bien español. ¿Dónde lo aprendiste?
B   En una escuela de idiomas en Salamanca. Estudié allí seis meses.
A   ¿Te gustó Salamanca?
B   Sí, me gustó mucho. Es una ciudad muy bonita.

una escuela de idiomas   *a school of languages*

Note the use of **gustar** in the Preterite tense: **me, te, le . . . gustó** (Salamanca). The third person plural is **gustaron: me, te, le . . . gustaron** (los españoles).

PRACTIQUE
A   *Complete these sentences with the correct Preterite form of the verbs in brackets.*
1 Luis (*estudiar*) español en Sevilla.
2 Yo (*viajar*) a Andalucía con unos amigos.

3 Mis amigos (*volver*) a Nueva York anteayer.
4 ¿Cuántos días (*pasar*) tú en Ibiza?
5 Ellos (*vivir*) dos años en Santiago de Chile.
6 Nosotros (*vender*) nuestro coche ayer.

anteayer *the day before yesterday*

B *Study this sequence of actions in the first person singular of the Preterite tense. Change each verb into the third person singular as if you were reporting what someone else did.*
Ejemplo: Me levanté a las 7.00.
            Se levantó a las 7.00.

1 *Me levanté* a las 7.00.
2 *Tomé* un café con leche.
3 *Salí* de casa a las 8.30.
4 *Cogí* el autobús.
5 *Comencé* a trabajar a las 9.00.
6 *Comí* a la 1.00 en una cafetería.
7 A las 2.00 *volví* al trabajo.
8 *Terminé* a las 5.00.
9 *Volví* a casa.
10 *Escuché* la radio, *escribí* una carta, *descansé* un momento y a las 8.30 *cené*.
11 *Me acosté* a las 11.00.

2 Irregular Preterite forms

Some verbs have an irregular Preterite. Here is a list of the most important.

andar (*to walk*)	anduve, anduviste, anduvo, anduvimos, anduvisteis, anduvieron.
estar (*to be*)	estuve, estuviste, estuvo, estuvimos, estuvisteis, estuvieron.
haber (*to have, aux.*)	hube, hubiste, hubo, hubimos, hubisteis, hubieron.
obtener (*to get*)	obtuve, obtuviste, obtuvo, obtuvimos, obtuvisteis, obtuvieron.
tener (*to have*)	tuve, tuviste, tuvo, tuvimos, tuvisteis, tuvieron.

saber (*to know*)	supe, supiste, supo, supimos, supisteis, supieron.
poner (*to put*)	puse, pusiste, puso, pusimos, pusisteis, pusieron.
suponer (*to suppose*)	supuse, supusiste, supuso, supusimos, supusisteis, supusieron.
dar (*to give*)	di, diste, dio, dimos, disteis, dieron.
decir (*to say*)	dije, dijiste, dijo, dijimos, dijisteis, dijeron.
hacer (*to do, make*)	hice, hiciste, hizo, hicimos, hicisteis, hicieron.
querer (*to want*)	quise, quisiste, quiso, quisimos, quisisteis, quisieron.
venir (*to come*)	vine, viniste, vino, vinimos, vinisteis, vinieron.
traer (*to bring*)	traje, trajiste, trajo, trajimos, trajisteis, trajeron.
ir (*to go*)	fui, fuiste, fue, fuimos, fuisteis, fueron.
ser (*to be*)	fui, fuiste, fue, fuimos, fuisteis, fueron.

¿Qué hiciste ayer?　*What did you do yesterday?*
Fui al estadio.　*I went to the stadium.*
Yo estuve en el campo.　*I was in the countryside.*

3　Spelling changes in the Preterite tense

Some verbs need a change in the spelling in the first person singular to enable the final consonant of the stem to keep the same sound as in the infinitive. Some of these verbs are:

llegar (*to arrive*)	llegué (*I arrived*)
pagar (*to pay*)	pagué (*I paid*)
sacar (*to get, e.g. tickets*)	saqué (*I got*)
tocar (*to play an instrument*)	toqué (*I played*)

A spelling change may also occur because of an accent in the infinitive or because there would otherwise be more than two vowels together.

caer (*to fall*)	caí, caíste, cayó, caímos, caísteis, cayeron.
leer (*to read*)	leí, leíste, leyó, leímos, leísteis, leyeron.
oír (*to hear*)	oí, oíste, oyó, oímos, oísteis, oyeron.

Diálogo 2: ¿Qué hiciste anoche? (*What did you do last night?*)
A ¿Qué hiciste anoche?
B Estuve en casa. Tuvimos invitados a cenar.
A Yo fui al teatro con Alfonso. Después fuimos a bailar. Llegué muy tarde a casa.

PRACTIQUE
C *Complete these sentences with the correct Preterite form of the verbs in brackets.*
1 Durante las vacaciones Gloria y yo (*andar*) mucho.
2 Ayer no salí porque (*tener que*) trabajar.
3 ¿Dónde (*poner*) Vd. las llaves?
4 Agustín (*dar*) una fiesta en su casa.
5 ¿Qué (*decir*) Paco?
6 ¿Qué (*hacer*) Vds. el sábado por la noche?

D *Say what you did on your last holiday.*
1 ¿Dónde pasó Vd. sus vacaciones?
2 ¿Con quién fue?
3 ¿Cuánto tiempo estuvo allí?
4 ¿Qué hizo durante las vacaciones? (*tomar el sol, bañarse, salir de excursión, dormir mucho, etc*).
5 ¿Le gustó el lugar?
6 ¿Cuándo volvió?

24 Saying what you used to do

1 Imperfect tense

To refer to a continuous or repeated action in the past (e.g. *I used to work in Spain, they used to come here every day*) we use the Imperfect tense. There are two sets of endings for this tense: one for **-ar** verbs and another one for verbs in **-er** and **-ir**. Here is the Imperfect tense of an **-ar** verb.

trabajar (*to work*)

trabaj**aba**	*I used to work/was working*
trabaj**abas**	*you used to work/were working* (fam.)
trabaj**aba**	*you, he, she used to work/you were/he, she was working*
trabaj**ábamos**	*we used to work/were working*
trabaj**abais**	*you used to work/were working* (fam.)
trabaj**aban**	*you, they used to work/were working*

Note that the first and third person singular share the same ending.

¿Dónde trabajaba Vd. antes?   *Where did you work before?*
Trabajaba en Bilbao.   *I used to work in Bilbao.*

These are the endings of regular **-er** and **-ir** verbs.

tener (*to have*)

ten**ía**		*I used to have*	
ten**ías**		*you used to have* (fam.)	
ten**ía**	un piso	*you/he/she used to have*	a flat
ten**íamos**		*we used to have*	
ten**íais**		*you used to have* (fam.)	
ten**ían**		*you/they used to have*	

vivir (*to live*)

vivía		*I used to live*	
vivías		*you used to live* (fam.)	
vivía	solo(s)	*you/he/she used to live*	*alone*
vivíamos		*we used to live*	
vivíais		*you used to live* (fam.)	
vivían		*you/they used to live*	

Note that the first and third person singular share the same endings and that all persons carry an accent.

> Fernando tenía un apartamento on the Costa del Sol.   *Fernando used to have an apartment on the Costa del Sol.*
> Nosotros teníamos un piso cerca de allí.   *We used to have a flat near there.*
> ¿Con quién vivías?   *Who did you live with?*
> Vivía solo.   *I used to live alone.*

2 Irregular Imperfect forms

There are only three irregular verbs in the Imperfect tense: **ir** (*to go*), **ser** (to be) and **ver** (*to see*).

ir	**ser**	**ver**
iba	era	veía
ibas	eras	veías
iba	era	veía
íbamos	éramos	veíamos
ibais	erais	veíais
iban	eran	veían

> Yo iba al cine todas las semanas.   *I used to go to the cinema every week.*
> Enrique era un buen amigo mío.   *Enrique was a good friend of mine.*
> La veíamos todos los días.   *We used to see her everyday.*

3 *Soler*

To say what we used to do we may also use the verb **soler** (*to be accustomed to, to be in the habit of*) in the Imperfect tense followed by an infinitive.

Solían venir todos los domingos.   *They used to come every Sunday.*

Carmen solía llegar a las 9.00.   *Carmen used to arrive at 9.00.*

***Diálogo:* Ganaba muy poco** (*I used to earn very little*)

A   ¿Dónde trabajabas antes?

B   Trabajaba en una fábrica.

A   ¿Por qué dejaste el trabajo?

B   Pues, ganaba muy poco y tenía que trabajar mucho. Entraba a las 8.00 y solía terminar a las 6.00.

PRACTIQUE

Juan Pérez was a very methodical man. This is what he used to do everyday before he retired. Complete the text with the Imperfect tense form of the infinitive in brackets.

Juan Pérez se levantaba a las 7.30, (*desayunar*) y (*salir*) de casa a las 8.30. (*Coger*) el autobús y (*llegar*) a la oficina a las 9.00. Primero (*leer*) las cartas y luego (*empezar*) a trabajar. No (*hablar*) con nadie. A la 1.30 (*dejar*) su trabajo e* (*ir*) a comer a un restaurante. Por la tarde (*trabajar*) de 3.00 a 6.00. A las 6.00 (*ponerse*) su chaqueta y (*volver*) a casa donde su mujer le (*esperar*) para merendar. Por la tarde (*leer*) el periódico y su mujer (*ver*) la televisión . . .

merendar   *to have an afternoon snack*

* (Note that **y** becomes **e** before a word beginning with an **i**.)

4   Imperfect and Preterite

The Imperfect tense is also used to refer to an action which was taking place when something else happened. Here it is often used in conjunction with the Preterite. (See also Unit 25, section **2**)

Yo **salía** de casa cuando ella **llegó**.   *I was leaving the house when she arrived.*

Terminábamos de comer cuando **ocurrió**.   *We were finishing our meal when it happened.*

Yo **conducía** el coche cuando la **ví**.   *I was driving the car when I saw her.*

25 Describing the past

1 Places, people and things

To describe places, people and things with reference to the past we normally use the Imperfect tense (see pp. 98–9). The verbs most frequently used in description are **ser** (see Unit 3), **estar** (see Unit 3), **tener** (see Unit 8) and the impersonal forms of **haber**, such as **hay** and **había** (see Unit 10). Remember that in description **ser** (*to be*) normally refers to general characteristics or features of a person, place or thing, whereas **estar** (*to be*) is used to indicate location or a temporary state or condition.

Describing a place
El hotel donde pasamos nuestras vacaciones **era** bastante grande. **Tenía** piscina, un restaurante y dos bares. **Estaba** a cinco minutos de la playa. Enfrente del hotel **había** una playa estupenda.

Describing a person
Mi abuelo **era** un hombre muy amable y simpático, de carácter alegre. **Era** alto, delgado y **tenía** el pelo muy blanco. **Llevaba** siempre un sombrero negro.

de carácter alegre *of a happy disposition*
el pelo *hair*
llevaba (llevar) *he used to wear (to wear)*

Describing a thing
El bolso que vi en la tienda **era** de cuero, de color marrón. No **era** ni grande ni pequeño. **Costaba** 8.000 pesetas.

era de cuero *it was made of leather*
ni . . . ni *neither . . . nor*

Diálogo ¿Cómo era su cartera? (*What was your briefcase like?*)
A Buenos días. Anoche dejé mi cartera aquí en la recepción. ¿La tiene Vd.?

100   *Describing the past*

B   ¿Cómo era su cartera, señor?
A   Era de cuero, de color negro. Estaba casi nueva.
B   ¿Qué llevaba Vd. dentro?
A   Llevaba mi pasaporte y otros documentos.
B   ¿Cómo se llama Vd., señor?
A   Mark Thompson.
B   Sí, señor Thompson. Aquí está su cartera.
A   Muchas gracias. Es Vd. muy amable.
B   De nada.

Llevaba (llevar)   *I was/you were carrying (to carry)*
dentro   *inside*
Es Vd. muy amable   *That's very kind of you*
la recepción   *reception*

PRACTIQUE
A   *Here is an apartment for sale. Describe it as if you had already seen it.*

VENDO APARTAMENTO EN PALMA DE MALLORCA
* 4 habitaciones
* 2 cuartos de baño
* terraza muy grande
* a 100 m. de la playa
* 4.000.000 de pesetas

1 ¿En qué ciudad estaba el apartamento?
2 ¿Cuántas habitaciones tenía?
3 ¿Cuántos cuartos de baño tenía?
4 ¿Cómo era la terraza?
5 ¿A cuántos metros de la playa estaba?
6 ¿Cuánto costaba?

2   Description within a narrative

In a narrative context, the Imperfect tense and the Preterite often appear together. While the first describes, the second narrates a series of actions or events. (See also Unit 24, section **4**.) Look at this text.

Salimos del hotel a las 8.00. **Hacía** mucho sol. **Llegamos** a Granada a las 10.00. Primero **visitamos** La Alhambra. **Había** mucha gente. **Eran** casi las 12.00 cuando **salimos** de allí . . .

PRACTIQUE

B *Choose the correct tense: the Preterite or the Imperfect.*

Aquella noche hacía mucho calor. Después de cenar yo (*salía/salí*) a la terraza. (*Eran/fueron*) casi las 11.00 de la noche y yo (*estaba/estuve*) muy cansado. (*Hubo/había*) poca gente en la calle. (*Bebía/bebí*) un café y (*fumé/fumaba*) un cigarrillo mientras (*escuché/escuchaba*) música. Alguien (*llamó/llamaba*) a la puerta. (*Fueron/eran*) Elena y Ricardo, dos amigos míos.

estar cansado   *to be tired*
mientras   *whilst*
llamar a la puerta   *to knock at the door*

26 How to link sentences

1 *Que*

The word most frequently used in Spanish to link sentences or parts of
a sentence is **que**. **Que** may refer to persons or things and it may be the
subject or the object of the verb. In this context it functions as a
relative pronoun and it translates into English as *who, whom, which* or
that.

> La chica **que** viene es mi prima. *The girl who is coming is my
> cousin.*
> La persona **que** busco no está aquí. *The person (whom) I'm
> looking for is not here.*
> El telegrama **que** envió Soledad está ahí. *The telegram which
> (that) Soledad sent is there.*
> La chaqueta **que** compré está en el armario. *The jacket which
> (or that) I bought is in the wardrobe.*

The relative pronoun cannot be omitted in Spanish as may happen in
English.

> *The person I am looking for . . .* La persona **que** busco : . .

2 *Quien, quienes*

Quien (*sing.*), **quienes** (*pl.*) are used for persons after a preposition.

> El chico **con quien** me viste es mi hermano. *The boy you saw me
> with is my brother.* (= *with whom*)
> Esa es la señora **de quien** te hablé. *That is the lady I told you
> about.* (= *of whom*)
> Las personas **a quienes** alquilamos la casa son españoles. *The
> people we rented the house to are Spanish.* (= *to whom*)

3 *El cual (el que), la cual (la que), los cuales (los que), las cuales (las que)*

Por, sin and longer prepositions such as *detrás de, delante de, junto a*, require the use of one of the above forms.

> Hay dos carreteras por **las cuales (las que)** se puede llegar a Burgos. *There are two main roads along which you can get to Burgos.*
>
> Perdí mi pasaporte **sin el cual (el que)** no pude viajar. *I lost my passport without which I could not travel.*
>
> Visitamos un pueblo **detrás del cual (del que)** había un viejo castillo. *We visited a village behind which there was an old castle.*

4 *Cuyo*

Cuyo is a relative adjective which is equivalent to the English word *whose* or *of which*. As an adjective it must agree with the noun. Therefore it can be singular or plural, masculine or feminine: **cuyo, cuya, cuyos, cuyas**.

> Ese es el señor **cuyo** piso está al lado del mío. *That is the gentleman whose flat is next to mine.*
>
> Estuvimos en un hotel **cuyas** habitaciones daban al mar. *We stayed in a hotel whose rooms faced the sea.*

In questions *Whose?* translates as **¿De quién?**

> **¿De quién** es esta maleta? *Whose is this suitcase?*
> **¿De quién es?** *Whose is it?*

5 *Donde/dónde*

Donde is used when a place is indicated.

> La calle **(en) donde** vivo es tranquila. *The street where I live is quiet.*
>
> La montaña **adonde** fuimos está muy lejos. *The mountain we went to is very far.*
>
> El pueblo **de donde** viene se llama Villalba. *The village where he comes from is called Villalba.*

Note the accent on **dónde** in the following examples where it follows a verb of communication or knowledge.

No sé **dónde** estas. *I don't know where you are.*

No me dijo **dónde** estaba. *He didn't tell me where he was.*

Diálogo: ¡**Claro que sí!** (*Certainly!*)

A ¿Quién es esa chica que está allí?

B ¿La que está en el balcón?

A Sí, la que está con aquel señor.

B Es Ana. Es la muchacha de quien te hablé. ¿Quieres conocerla?

A ¡Claro que sí!

PRACTIQUE

Complete these sentences with the correct word: **donde, quienes, que, quien, la cual, el cual.**

1 El señor . . . . . está allí es mi padre.

2 Visitamos la catedral junto a . . . . . estaba el museo.

3 La casa . . . . . vivimos es muy confortable.

4 ¿Es ése el muchacho de . . . . . me hablaste?

5 Tuve que obtener un visado sin . . . . . no podía ir.

6 Los chicos con . . . . . estaba son ingleses.

el muchacho *boy*   **el visado** *visa*

6 Other linking words

Sentences can also be linked by means of words such as **porque** (*because*), **pues** (*as, since, because*), **como** (*how, as*), **cuando** (*when*).

Porque

¿Por qué no vas a Andalucía? *Why don't you go to Andalucía?*

No voy porque ya conozco Andalucía. *I don't go because I already know Andalucía.*

Pues

Necesito tu ayuda pues tú conoces el camino. *I need your help as you know the way.*

No pude salir pues vino José Luis. *I couldn't go out because José Luis came.*

Como/cómo

No sé cómo está. *I don't know how she is.*

No me dijo cómo estaba. *He didn't tell me how he was.*

Puedes venir como quieras. *You can come as you like.*

Cuando/cuándo

¿Sabes cuándo llega Carmen? *Do you know when Carmen is arriving?*

No sé cuándo llegará. *I don't know when she'll arrive.*

Note: In the sentences above, **como** and **cuando** carry an accent when they come after a verb which indicates knowledge or communication.

27 Saying what you have done

1 Perfect tense

To say what we have done or what has happened (e.g. *I have finished, It has started to rain*) we use the Perfect tense. This tense refers to completed actions carried out in the past but associated in some way with the present. It is often accompanied by expressions such as **alguna vez** (*ever*), **nunca** (*never*), **todavía** (*still, yet*), **ya** (*already*), **hoy** (*today*), **esta mañana** (*this morning*), **este mes** (*this month*), **este año** (*this year*). To form the Perfect tense we use the Present tense of **haber** (*to have*) followed by a past participle which is invariable. Remember that the past participle of -**ar** verbs ends in -**ado** while -**er** and -**ir** verbs form the past participle by adding -**ido** to the stem. See Unit 17 for regular past participles and Unit 21 for irregular ones.

he termin**ado**	*I have finished*
has termin**ado**	*you have finished* (fam.)
ha termin**ado**	*you have, he/she has finished*
hemos termin**ado**	*we have finished*
habéis termin**ado**	*you have finished* (fam.)
han termin**ado**	*you/they have finished*

¿Has terminado ya?   *Have you finished already?*
Todavía no he terminado.   *I haven't finished yet.*
¿Has comido en ese restaurante alguna vez?   *Have you ever eaten in that restaurant?*
No he comido nunca allí.   *I have never eaten there.*

2 Perfect or Preterite

As in English, the Perfect tense sometimes overlaps with the Preterite. In the examples which follow either tense is correct.

¿Desayunaste?	*Did you have breakfast?*
¿Has desayunado?	*Have you had breakfast?*
¿Compraste el pan?	*Did you buy the bread?*
¿Has comprado el pan?	*Have you bought the bread?*

The tendency in Spanish is to use the Perfect tense when the verb refers to the recent past whereas the Preterite is preferred to indicate a more distant action in the past. Here are some further examples of the use of the Perfect tense.

He salido de casa a las 9.00. *I have left the house at 9.00.*
En el tren he visto a Juan. *I've seen Juan on the train.*
He llegado al trabajo a la hora. *I've arrived at work on time.*

3 Pronouns with the Perfect tense

If there are any pronouns in the sentence these must go before **haber.**

Lo hemos terminado.	*We have finished it.*
Se han marchado.	*They have gone.*
Le he visto hoy.	*I've seen him today.*

Diálogo: **Todavía no ha empezado** (*It hasn't started yet*)

A Buenas tardes. ¿Ha empezado la película?
B No, señorita. Todavía no ha empezado. Empieza dentro de cinco minutos.
A Gracias.

Note: **todavía** may be replaced by **aún** which has the same meaning.

PRACTIQUE

A *Answer each of these questions affirmatively or negatively, as suggested.*

Ejemplo: ¿Ha leído Vd. este libro?
Sí, ya lo he leído. *o*
No, todavía (aún) no lo he leído.

1 ¿Ha preparado Vd. la cena? (Sí)
2 ¿Has recibido la carta? (No)
3 ¿Has limpiado la habitación? (No)
4 ¿Habéis reservado los billetes? (Sí)

5 ¿Han escuchado ellos este disco?   (No)
6 ¿Han encontrado Vds. las maletas?   (Sí)

B *Complete these sentences with the correct Perfect tense form from the list.*

1 Yo . . . . . dos cartas hoy.
2 El banco . . . . . a las 9.00.
3 Esta tarde nosotros . . . . .
   a Angel.
4 Mi abuela . . . . . Tenía 85 años.
5 Yo te lo . . . . . muchas veces.
   Es importante.
6 ¿Y tú qué . . . . . hoy?

hemos visto
he dicho
ha abierto
has hecho
ha muerto
he escrito

28 Saying what you had done

1 Pluperfect tense

To say what we had done or what had happened (e.g. *I had finished, It had started to rain*) we use the Pluperfect tense. This is formed with the Imperfect form of **haber** followed by a past participle which is invariable, as for the Perfect tense (see Unit 27).

había termin**ado**	*I had finished*
habías termin**ado**	*you had finished* (fam.)
había termin**ado**	*you/he/she had finished*
habíamos termin**ado**	*we had finished*
habíais termin**ado**	*you had finished* (fam.)
habían termin**ado**	*you/they had finished*

¿Habías visto esto antes?   *Had you seen this before?*
Nunca lo había visto.   *I had never seen it.*
Nunca habíamos estado aquí.   *We had never been here.*

2 Use of Pluperfect with Preterite

In time clauses the Pluperfect is often linked to the Preterite, as shown in the examples below.

La reunión había terminado cuando llegué.   *The meeting had finished when I arrived.*
Cuando salimos había dejado de llover.   *When we went out it had stopped raining.*

Diálogo: **¿Por qué no habías venido?** (*Why hadn't you come?*)
A   Hola Fernando. ¿Qué hay? ¿Por qué no habías venido?
B   No había podido. He tenido mucho trabajo.
A   Me alegro mucho de verte.

   B Yo también.
   A ¿Sabes quién está aquí?
   B ¿Quién?
   A Julia.
   B ¿Julia? No sabía que había vuelto de España.
   A Sí, volvió la semana pasada.

la semana pasada *last week*

PRACTIQUE
Complete these sentences with the Pluperfect tense form of the verb in brackets.
Ejemplo: Cuando llegué la reunión (*comenzar*).
          Cuando llegué la reunión había comenzado.
1 Cuando volví Antonio (*salir*).
2 Cuando entramos la fiesta (*empezar*).
3 Cuando llamaste Marta (*marcharse*).
4 Cuando salimos ellos ya (*volver*).
5 Cuando llegó tú ya (*acostarse*).
6 Cuando nos levantamos la lluvia (*parar*).

parar *to stop*

29 Talking about the Future

1 Future tense

The tense most frequently associated with future reference is the Future tense. To form the Future tense you use the infinitive form followed by the ending, which is the same for the three conjugations. Here is the Future form of three regular verbs representing each of the three conjugations.

estar (*to be*)

estar**é**		*I will be*	
estar**ás**		*you will be* (fam.)	
estar**á**	en Granada	*you/he/she will be*	*in Granada*
estar**emos**		*we will be*	
estar**éis**		*you will be* (fam.)	
estar**án**		*you/they will be*	

¿Dónde estarás este verano?   *Where will you be this summer?*
Estaré en Granada.   *I'll be in Granada.*

volver (*to return*)

volver**é**		*I will return*	
volver**ás**		*you will return* (fam.)	
volver**á**	mañana	*you/he/she will return*	*tomorrow*
volver**emos**		*we will return*	
volver**éis**		*you will return* (fam.)	
volver**án**		*you/they will return*	

¿Cuándo volveréis?   *When will you return?*
Volveremos el año que viene.   *We'll return next year.*

ir (*to go*)

ir**é**		*I will go*	
ir**ás**		*you will go* (fam.)	
ir**á**	a México	*you/he/she will go*	*to Mexico*
ir**emos**		*we will go*	
ir**éis**		*you will go* (fam.)	
ir**án**		*you/they will go*	

¿Adónde irán Vds. este año?   *Where will you go this year?*
Iremos a México.   *We'll go to Mexico.*

Note that only the first person plural does not carry an accent.

Diálogo 1: Pasaré a buscarlo esta tarde (*I'll come and get it this afternoon*)
A   Buenas tardes.
B   Buenas tardes, señora. ¿Qué desea?
A   ¿Puede repararme este neumático, por favor?
B   Sí, cómo no. Estará listo dentro de una hora.
A   De acuerdo. Pasaré a buscarlo esta tarde. Adiós.
B   Adiós.

¿Qué desea?   *Can I help you?*   **el neumático**   *tyre*
reparar   *to repair*   **Sí, cómo no**   *certainly*

PRACTIQUE
A   *Look at this extract from a letter where the verbs are missing. Complete it with the appropriate verb in the Future tense:* **coger, quedarse, llegar, estar, ir, llevar**.

Todo está listo para mi viaje. Yo . . . . . al aeropuerto de Málaga a las 11.00. Desde allí . . . . . en tren hasta Fuengirola donde . . . . . un autobús para Marbella. A la 1.00 más o menos . . . . . en Marbella. No . . . . . mucho equipaje porque sólo . . . . . una semana.

el aeropuerto   *airport*

2 Irregular Future forms

Some verbs have an irregular stem in the Future tense but the endings are the same as those of regular verbs. Here is a list of the most important.

decir (*to say*)	diré, dirás, dirá, diremos, diréis, dirán
haber (*to have,* aux.)	habré, habrás, habrá, habremos, habréis, habrán.
hacer (*to do, make*)	haré, harás, hará, haremos, haréis, harán.
obtener (*to obtain*)	obtendré, obtendrás, obtendrá, obtendremos, obtendréis, obtendrán
poner (*to put*)	pondré, pondrás, pondrá, pondremos, pondréis, pondrán
querer (*to want*)	querré, querrás, querrá, querremos, querréis, querrán
saber (*to know*)	sabré, sabrás, sabrá, sabremos, sabréis, sabrán
salir (*to go out, leave*)	saldré, saldrás, saldrá, saldremos, saldréis, saldrán
tener (*to have*)	tendré, tendrás, tendrá, tendremos, tendréis, tendrán
venir (*to come*)	vendré, vendrás, vendrá, vendremos, vendréis, vendrán

Diálogo 2: ¿**Qué harás?** (*What will you do?*)

A   ¿Qué harás esta tarde?
B   Saldré con Laura. Iremos a la piscina.
     Vendrás con nosotros, ¿verdad?
A   No podré. Tendré que ir al aeropuerto a esperar a mi madre.

PRACTIQUE

B *Answer each of these questions saying when you will do what is asked.*

Ejemplo: ¿Has hecho el trabajo?   (esta tarde)
        No, pero lo haré esta tarde.

1 ¿Has hecho la habitación?   (pronto)
2 ¿Has obtenido el visado?   (pasado mañana)

3 ¿Se lo has dicho a Jorge?   (esta noche)
4 ¿Has puesto la mesa?   (ahora)
5 ¿Te has puesto la camisa nueva?   (el domingo)
6 ¿Has hecho las maletas?   (por la mañana)

hacer la habitación   *to do the room*   **ponerse (la camisa)**   *to put on*
hacer las maletas   *to pack*   *(the shirt)*

3   *Ir a* + infinitive

English also expresses futurity by using the verb *to go* with an infintive (*I'm going to buy a car*). Spanish also uses a similar construction with **ir a** followed by an **infinitive** (see Unit 18, page 71).

¿Qué vas a hacer este año?   *What are you going to do this year?*
Voy a estudiar español.   *I'm going to study Spanish.*
Vamos a trabajar.   *We're going to work.*

4   Present tense expressing the future

As in English, Spanish also uses the Present tense to refer to the future, particularly with verbs which indicate movement, but also with the verb **hacer**.

Mañana vamos a Zaragoza.   *Tomorrow we're going to Zaragoza.*
Salimos mañana por la tarde.   *We leave tomorrow afternoon.*
Volvemos el sábado próximo (o el sábado que viene).   *We come back next Saturday.*
¿Qué haces este fin de semana?   *What are you doing this weekend?*

30 Saying what you would do

1 Conditional tense

To say what we would do or what would happen (e.g. *I would go, it would break*) we use the Conditional tense. Like the Future it is formed with the infinitive, to which the endings are added. The endings of the three conjugations are the same as those of the Imperfect tense of -er and -ir verbs (see Unit 24). Here is the Conditional tense of three regular verbs representing each of the three conjugations.

estar (*to be*)

estar**ía**		*I would be*	
estar**ías**		*you would be* (fam.)	
estar**ía**	en Perú	*you/he/she would be*	*in Peru*
estar**íamos**		*we would be*	
estar**íais**		*you would be* (fam.)	
estar**ían**		*you/they would be*	

Dijo que estaría listo mañana. *He said it would be ready tomorrow.*

Me dijeron que estarían aquí a las 6.00. *They told me they would be here at 6.00.*

volver (*to return*)

volver**ía**		*I would return*	
volver**ías**		*you would return* (fam.)	
volver**ía**	pronto	*you/he/she would return*	*soon*
volver**íamos**		*we would return*	
volver**íais**		*you would return* (fam.)	
volver**ían**		*you/they would return*	

Pablo dijo que volvería pronto. *Pablo said he would return soon.*

116   *Saying what you would do*

¿A qué hora volverías?   *What time would you return?*

ir (*to go*)

iría		*I would go*	
irías		*you would go* (fam.)	
iría	a Sevilla	*you/he/she would go*	to Seville
iríamos		*we would go*	
iríais		*you would go* (fam.)	
irían		*you/they would go*	

Yo iría a Sevilla, pero no hay vuelos.   *I would go to Seville, but there are no flights.*

Dijeron que irían en el coche.   *They said they would go by car.*

2 Conditional tense in indirect speech

Note that the Conditional is often used in indirect speech to report what somebody said. The verb most frequently used in indirect speech is **decir**, normally found in the Present tense or in any of the past tenses. Look at the way these direct statements have been transformed into indirect speech.

Direct:

  'Iré mañana'.   *'I'll go tomorrow.'*

Indirect:

  Dice que irá mañana.   *He says he will go tomorrow.*

  (Main verb in the Present tense followed by Future.)

  Dijo que iría mañana.   *He said he would go tomorrow.*

  (Main verb in the Preterite followed by Conditional.)

Diálogo 1: **Me gustaría hablar con él** (*I'd like to talk to him*)

A   ¿Ha llegado Eduardo?

B   No, todavía no. Dijo que iría primero al banco y que estaría aquí a las dos.

A   Quiero verle. Me gustaría hablar con él.

A   *Transform these sentences into indirect speech.*

Ejemplo: 'Viajaré en avión.' (Ana Luisa dijo . . .)

      Ana Luisa dijo que *viajaría* en avión.

1 '*Compraré* aquel coche.' (Mi padre dijo . . .)
2 '*Alquilaremos* el piso.' (Mis amigos dijeron . . .)
3 '*Me marcharé* pronto.' (Gloria dijo . . .)
4 '*Nos levantaremos* a las 7.00.' (Ellos dijeron . . .)
5 '*Pasaré* un mes en San Francisco.' (Tú dijiste . . .)
6 '*Les acompañaré.*' (Yo les dije . . .)

acompañar   *to accompany*

3   Irregular Conditional forms

Verbs which have irregular stems in the Future tense also have them in the Conditional. The endings are the same as those of regular verbs. The first and second person singular and the first person plural will serve to illustrate this point. Remember that the third person singular is the same as the first.

decir (*to say*)	diría, dirías . . . diríamos . . .
haber (*to have*)	habría, habrías . . . habríamos . . .
hacer (*to do, make*)	haría, harías . . . haríamos . . .
obtener (*to obtain*)	obtendría, obtendrías . . . obtendríamos . . .
poner (*to put*)	pondría, pondrías . . . pondríamos . . .
querer (*to want*)	querría, querrías . . . querríamos . . .
saber (*to know*)	sabría, sabrías . . . sabríamos . . .
salir (*to go out*)	saldría, saldrías . . . saldríamos . . .
tener (*to have*)	tendría, tendrías . . . tendríamos . . .
venir (*to come*)	vendría, vendrías . . . vendríamos . . .

José dijo que habría una fiesta en su casa.   *José said (that) there would be a party in his house.*
¿Qué diría tu madre?   *What would your mother say?*
¿Qué harías tú en mi caso?   *What would you do in my case?*

***Diálogo 2:* Podríamos ir a la playa** (*We could go to the beach*)
A   ¿Crees que hará sol mañana?
B   En la radio dijeron que haría buen tiempo.
A   Podríamos ir a la playa. ¿Qué te parece?
B   Sí, sería una buena idea.

una buena idea   *a good idea*

PRACTIQUE

B   *Complete these sentences with the appropriate verb from the list.*

1   No sé que . . . . . yo sin ti.   podrías
2   ¿Tú . . . . . llevarme en el coche?   tendrían que
3   Ellos . . . . . antes de las 7.00.   haría
4   Yo le . . . . . la verdad.   saldrían
5   Dijeron que ellos . . . . . volver a España.   vendría
6   Victoria dijo que ella . . . . . a vernos hoy.   diría

4   Conditional Perfect tense

To say what you would have done or what would have happened (e.g.
I would have gone, it would have broken) we use the Conditional
Perfect. This is formed with the Conditional of **haber** followed by a
past participle, which is invariable. See Unit 17 for regular past
participles and Unit 21 for irregular ones.

estudiar (*to study*)

habría estud**iado**	*I would have studied*
habrías estud**iado**	*you would have studied* (fam.)
habría estud**iado**	*you/he/she would have studied*
habríamos estud**iado**	*we would have studied*
habríais estud**iado**	*you would have studied* (fam.)
habrían estud**iado**	*you/they would have studied*

Yo habría estudiado español.   *I would have studied Spanish.*
¿Qué habrías hecho tú?   *What would you have done?*
Yo se lo habría dicho.   *I would have told him.*

Diálogo 3: **Yo no habría podido** (*I wouldn't have been able to*)
A   ¿Qué habrías hecho tú en mi caso?
B   Le habría dicho la verdad. Habría sido mejor.
A   Yo no habría podido.

PRACTIQUE

C   *Say what you would have done.*
Ejemplo: No lo compró.
             Yo lo habría comprado.

1 No lo hizo.
2 No se lo dijo.
3 No la invitó.
4 No se lo dio.
5 No les escribió.
6 No lo leyó.

31 Expressing obligation and necessity

1 *Tener que*

English expresses obligation and necessity in various ways (e.g. *I have to go, I must do it, one has to work, one needs to study, I need to be there soon*). Spanish also uses different constructions. Of these, the most frequent one is **tener que** with an infinitive. For the Present tense of **tener** see Unit 8. For **tener que** plus infinitive see Unit 18.

Tengo que salir.	*I have to (must) go out.*
Tuvimos que hacerlo.	*We had to do it.*
Tendrás que volver.	*You'll have to (must) return.*
Vd. tendría que decírselo.	*You'd have to (must) tell him.*

2 *Deber*

Deber is normally used to indicate moral obligation. It is conjugated like any other regular **-er** verb. In the Present tense it translates into English as *should* or *ought to*.

No debes fumar.	*You shouldn't (ought not to) smoke.*
Vd. debe descansar más.	*You should (ought to) rest more.*

In the past it translates as *ought to have* or *should have* followed by a past participle.

Debiste decírselo.	*You should (ought to) have told him.*
Debí comprarlo.	*I should (ought to) have bought it.*

Deber is often used in the Conditional followed by a plain infinitive or a perfect infinitive (**haber** + past participle).

Deberías perdonarla.	*You should forgive her.*
Deberías haberla perdonado.	*You should have forgiven her.*

3 *Hay que*

Hay que is an impersonal form and as such it cannot be used to refer to specific persons. It translates into English as *one has to, one must, one should, one needs to, it is necessary.* It varies according to tense. For **haber** see verb tables, p. 159.

Hay que trabajar.	*One has to work.*
Hubo que hacerlo.	*It was necessary to do it.*
Había que probarlo.	*One had to try it.*
Habrá que seguir.	*It will be necessary to continue.*
Habría que explicarlo.	*One would have to explain it.*

4 *Ser necesario, necesitar*

To indicate that something is considered necessary we may also use the impersonal construction **ser necesario** (*to be necessary*) followed by an infinitive.

Es necesario ganar.	*It's necessary to win.*
Fue necesario correr.	*It was necessary to run.*
Era necesario acabar.	*It was necessary to finish.*
Será necesario telefonear.	*It will be necessary to telephone.*

Necesitar (*to need*) is conjugated like any other regular **-ar** verb.

Necesita firmar.	*You need to sign.*
Necesitaba preguntarles.	*I needed to ask them.*

Diálogo 1: **Tendrá que estar . . .** (*You'll have to be . . .*)

A ¿A qué hora sale el vuelo para México?

B Sale a las 9.00 de la mañana. Pero tendrá que estar una hora antes en el aeropuerto.

A ¿A las 8.00 de la manana?

B Sí, señor. Hay que estar allí a las 8.00.

Diálogo 2: **Necesita visado** (*You need a visa*)

A　(*Al teléfono*) Consulado de Venezuela, ¿diga?

B　Buenos días. ¿Podría decirme si es necesario tener visado para viajar a Venezuela?

A　¿Qué pasaporte tiene Vd.?

B　Británico.

A　Sí, necesita visado. Tiene que traer su pasaporte y tres fotos.

B　¿Hay que traer el billete también?

A　No, no hace falta.

Note: **Hacer falta** (*to need, to be necessary*) is often used in the third person singular in an impersonal way:

Hace falta tener visado.　*You need (to have) a visa.*

PRACTIQUE

A　*Complete these sentences with the appropriate verb form.*

1 ¿Qué . . . . hacer tú esta tarde?	tendréis que
2 . . . . . . ir al médico. No me siento bien.	tuvo que
3 . . . . . . volver antes de nuestras vacaciones, pues mi madre se puso enferma.	tienes que
	tuvimos que
4 . . . . . . estudiar más español. No estudiáis lo suficiente.	tuvieron que
	tendré que
5 No encontraron hotel y . . . . irse a un camping.	
6 El coche de Carmen estaba estropeado. . . . . llevarlo al garaje.	

se puso (ponerse) enferma　*she became ill (to become)*
lo suficiente　*sufficiently, enough*
está estropeado　*it's out of order, not working*

B　*Translate these sentences into Spanish.*

1 We had to wait for two hours.

2 They will have to return tomorrow.

3 I shouldn't eat bread.

4 One has to study.

5 Is it necessary to book a table?

6 I need to see her.

32 Giving directions and instructions

1 Present tense

Directions and instructions can be given in a variety of ways. The simplest way is by using the Present tense, as you might do in English.

Directions

> Para ir a la Plaza España Vd. **dobla** a la derecha y **sigue** todo recto por esa calle hasta el final. *To go to Plaza España you turn right and carry straight on to the end of that street.*

Instructions

> Primero **vas** a Correos y **me traes** diez sellos de 45 pesetas, luego **me compras** . . . *First you go to the post-office and bring me ten 45-peseta stamps, then you buy me . . .*

2 *Tener que* + infinitive

Directions and instructions may also be given with **tener que** + infinitive. (For other uses of **tener que** see Unit 31.)

> Para ir a la Plaza de Cataluña tienes que tomar la Linea 1. *To go to Plaza de Cataluña you have to take Line 1.*
>
> Para conseguir el visado Vd. tiene que traer su pasaporte y tres fotos. *To get the visa you must bring your passport and three photos.*

3 Imperative forms

The verb form most frequently associated with directions and instructions is the Imperative (e.g. *turn left, come back, do it*). In Spanish we use different Imperative forms depending on who we are talking to (formal or familiar) and whether we are speaking to one or more than one person (singular or plural). To form the command or Imperative we use the stem of the first person singular of the Present tense. Here are the formal commands of three regular verbs representing each of the three conjugations: **doblar** (*to turn*), **ceder el paso** (*to give way*), **subir** (*to go up*).

Present (*first person*)	*Command*
doblo	dobl**e** (sing.)
	dobl**en** (pl.)
cedo el paso	ced**a** (sing.)
	ced**an** (pl.)
subo	sub**a** (sing.)
	sub**an** (pl.)

The negative command is formed by placing **no** before the verb.

> Doble a la derecha.   *Turn right.*
> No doble a la izquierda.   *Don't turn left.*
> Ceda el paso.   *Give way.*
> Suba por esta calle.   *Go up along this street.*

Note that first conjugation verbs (**-ar**) acquire the endings of second conjugation verbs (**-er**) while second and third conjugation verbs (**-er** and **-ir**) acquire the endings of the first conjugation.

Diálogo 1: **Siga Vd. todo recto** (*Go straight on*)
A   Perdone. ¿Dónde está la Calle Mayor, por favor?
B   Mire, siga Vd. todo recto hasta el final. Esa es la Calle Mayor.
A   Gracias.
B   De nada.

hasta   *as far as, until*

Notice the use of **Vd.** in **Siga Vd.** todo recto. This softens the command form and makes it more polite.

Diálogo 2: **Llénelo, por favor** (*Fill it up, please*)
A   Buenos días. Llénelo, por favor.
B   ¿Normal o super?
A   Normal. Y haga el favor de revisar el aceite.
B   De acuerdo.

¿**normal o super?** = *2-star or 4-star?* **revisar el aceite** *to check the oil*
haga el favor . . . *will you please . . .*

PRACTIQUE
A *Complete the following sentences with an appropriate verb from the list.*

1 . . . . . . a la izquierda.   Cruce
2 . . . . . . todo recto.   Tome
3 . . . . . . la plaza.   Haga
4 . . . . . . la Línea 2.   Siga
5 . . . . . . el paso.   Doble
6 . . . . . . el favor.   Ceda

4 Irregular Imperative forms

As the Imperative is formed with the stem of the first person singular of the Present tense, verbs which are irregular in the Present are also irregular in the Imperative. Here are some examples:

Infinitive	*Present*	*Imperative (sing./(pl.))*
conducir (*to drive*)	conduzco	**conduzca(n)**
cerrar (*to close*)	cierro	**cierre(n)**
volver (*to return*)	vuelvo	**vuelva(n)**
pedir (*to ask*)	pido	**pida(n)**
seguir (*to follow*)	sigo	**siga(n)**
hacer (*to do, make*)	hago	**haga(n)**
poner (*to put*)	pongo	**ponga(n)**

Ir (*to go*), **saber** (*to know*) and **ser** (*to be*) form the Imperative in a different way.

Infinitive	*Present*	*Imperative (sing./ (pl.))*
ir (*to go*)	voy	**vaya(n)**
saber (*to know*)	sé	**sepa(n)**
ser (*to be*)	soy	**sea(n)**

Note also the spelling changes necessary in verbs ending in **-car**, **-gar**:
busco (*I look for*) – bus**que** (*look for*), pago (*I pay*) – pa**gue** (*pay*).

5 Pronouns with Imperative

If the command includes a pronoun this must go at the end of the positive form but before the negative one. Positive commands which carry a pronoun may need to add an accent. Here are some examples:

Diga.	*Tell* (from **decir**, *to tell, say*).
Dígale.	*Tell him.*
No le diga.	*Don't tell him.*
Traiga.	*Bring* (from **traer**, to *bring*).
Tráigalo.	*Bring it.*
No lo traiga.	*Don't bring it.*

PRACTIQUE

B *For each of the instructions below write another one using the formal Imperative form.*

Ejemplo: Tiene que esperar un momento.
　　　　　Espere un momento.

1 Tiene que *traer* su pasaporte.
2 Hagan el favor de *venir* mañana.
3 Primero *va* a Correos y *me compra* cinco sellos de 60 pesetas.
4 Tiene que *telefonear* y *reservar* la habitación.
5 Haga el favor de no *fumar*.
6 Tienen que *volver* a las 5.00.

6 Familiar Commands

Familiar commands have different positive and negative forms. These are the positive familiar commands of three regular verbs representing each of the three conjugations: **doblar** (*to turn*), **ceder** el paso (*to give way*) **subir** (*to go up*).

Present (first person)	Positive command
doblo (*I turn*)	dobl**a** (sing.)
	dobl**ad** (pl.)
cedo el paso (*I give way*)	ced**e** (sing.)
	ced**ed** (pl.)
sub (*I go up*)	sub**e** (sing.)
	sub**id** (pl.)

Notice that the singular familiar command (positive form) is the same as the third person singular of the Present tense.

Here are the negative familiar commands for each of the three conjugations.

Present Indicative *(first person)*	*Negative command*
doblo	**no** doble**s** (sing.)
	no dobl**éis** (pl.)
cedo	**no** ced**as** (sing.)
	no ced**áis** (pl.)
subo	**no** sub**as** (sing.)
	no sub**áis** (pl.)

> No dobles aquí. Dobla en la esquina.   *Don't turn here. Turn at the corner.*
> No subas a pie. Sube en el ascensor.   *Don't walk up. Go up in the lift.*

7 Irregular familiar commands

The following verbs form the singular positive familiar command in an irregular way.

decir (*to say*)	**di**	Dile. *Tell him.*
hacer (*to do, make*)	**haz**	Hazlo. *Do it.*
ir (*to go*)	**ve**	Ve allí. *Go there.*
oir (*to hear*)	**oye**	¡Oye! *Listen!*
poner (*to put*)	**pon**	Ponlo aquí. *Put it here.*
salir (*to go out*)	**sal**	¡Sal! *Get out!*
ser (*to be*)	**sé**	Sé bueno. *Be good.*
tener (*to have*)	**ten**	Ten. *Here you are.*
venir (*to come*)	**ven**	Ven aquí. *Come here.*

Plural forms are regular.

8 'Let's' + verb

The Imperative form equivalent to the English phrase *Let's* takes the same ending as the formal command for **Vd.** plus **-mos** for **nosotros**.

doble (*turn*)	dob**lemos**	(*let's turn*)
ceda (*give way*)	ced**amos**	(*let's give way*)
suba (*go up*)	sub**amos**	(*let's go up*)

For **ir** we normally use the word **vamos** (*let's go*) instead of **vayamos**.

Diálogo 3: Ayúdame (*Help me*)

A ¿Carlos?
B Sí, dime.
A Ayúdame a bajar las maletas, por favor. Están muy pesadas.
B Sí, espera un momento. Voy en seguida.
A Lleva tú ésta y yo llevaré la otra.
B De acuerdo. ¿Dónde la pongo?
A Ponla en el coche.
B ¿En el asiento?
A No, no la pongas en el asiento. Ponla en el maletero.

bajar *to bring down*		**el asiento** *seat*
están pesadas *they're heavy*		**el maletero** *boot*
voy en seguida *I'll go straight away*		

PRACTIQUE

C *Read this extract from a letter giving directions. Then change the formal commands to the familiar form.*

Al llegar al aeropuerto *coja* un tren hasta la estacíon de Sants. En Sants *coja* la Línea l del metro y *bájese* en la Estación Fontana. Al salir de la estación *doble* a la izquierda y *siga* todo recto por esa calle hasta el primer semáforo. Allí *doble* a la izquierda otra vez, *cruce* la calle y encontrará el número 22.

bájese (bajarse) *get off*   **otra vez** *again*
el semáforo *traffic light*

Subjunctive mood

So far in this book all the tenses have been in the Indicative mood, e.g. Present Indicative. But there is another set of tenses in Spanish which correspond to the Subjunctive mood. Their forms and uses are different from those of the Indicative. In this Unit we shall deal with the Present Subjunctive and some of its uses. The next two Units will explain and illustrate three other Subjunctive tenses: the Perfect Subjunctive, the Imperfect and the Pluperfect.

The subjunctive is not normally used by itself. It usually forms part of a subordinate clause introduced by **que**, which is dependent on a main clause. The main clause sometimes carries the type of verb which calls for the use of the subjunctive in the subordinate clause. This is the case with verbs which indicate hope (e.g., *I hope he comes*), doubt (e.g., *I don't think he'll come*) or wishes and indirect commands e.g., *I want him to come, I want you to come*).

Espero que él venga. *I hope he comes.*

espero: main clause verb indicating hope.
que él venga: subordinate clause, with verb in the subjunctive. Because **espero** is in the Present tense (indicative) **venir** must be in the Present Subjunctive.

Notice also that the subject of the main clause is different from that of the subordinate clause: **Yo** espero que **él** venga. This is important because otherwise we don't need the subjunctive. We would use an infinitive instead.

Espero venir.   *I hope to come.*
Ella espera ir.   *She hopes to go.*

Here are some more examples of the uses of the subjunctive.

Esperamos que el buen tiempo dure unos días.   *We hope the good weather will last a few days.*

Quiero que me acompañes.   *I want you to come with me.*
No creo que ella tenga ninguna dificultad.   *I don't think she ha*
(or she'll have) any difficulty.

In the last example, if we eliminate the word **no**, the subordinate n
longer needs the subjunctive, as there is more certainty than in th
negative sentence.

Creo que ella tiene dificultades.   *I think she has difficulties.*

2   Present Subjunctive – formation

Like the Imperative (see Unit 32) the Present Subjunctive is forme
from the first person singular of the Present Indicative, e.g. **habl**
(hablar—*to speak*), **aprendo** (aprender—*to learn*), **escribo** (escribir–
to write). You drop the -o and add the corresponding endings: one se
of endings for first conjugation verbs and another for the second an
third conjugation. The first and third person singular of the Presen
Subjunctive correspond in form to formal commands (see Unit 3
page 124).

hablar (*to speak*)	**aprender** (*to learn*)	**escribir** (*to write*)
hable	aprenda	escriba
hables	aprendas	escribas
hable	aprenda	escriba
hablemos	aprendamos	escribamos
habléis	aprendáis	escribáis
hablen	aprendan	escriban

Quiero que tú hables con él.   *I want you to speak to him.*
María espera que yo aprenda español.   *Maria hopes that*
should learn Spanish.
Espero que me escribas.   *I hope you write to me.*

3   Irregular forms of Present Subjunctive

As with commands, verbs which are irregular in the first perso
singular of the Present Indicative are also irregular in the Presen
Subjunctive. Here is an example:

Infinitive		*Present Ind./1st person*
decir (*to say*)		**digo** (*I say*)

Present Subjunctive

digo	**digamos**	Quiero que me digas qué pasó. *I want you to tell me what happened.*
digas	**digáis**	
diga	**digan**	

For a list of irregular verbs in the Present Indicative see Unit 16.

Some verbs are irregular in a different way in the Present Subjunctive.

dar (*to give*)	dé, des, dé,
	demos, deis, den.
estar (*to be*)	esté, estés, esté,
	estemos, estéis, estén.
haber (*to have*)	haya, hayas, haya,
	hayamos, hayáis, hayan.
ir (*to go*)	vaya, vayas, vaya,
	vayamos, vayáis, vayan
saber (*to know*)	sepa, sepas, sepa,
	sepamos, sepáis, sepan.
ser (*to be*)	sea, seas, sea,
	seamos, seáis, sean.

The first and third person singular of **dar** must carry an accent in order to distinguish them from the preposition **de**. The accents in the Present Subjunctive of **estar** are the same as in the Present Indicative: **estás, está, estáis, están.**

Diálogo 1: **Quiero que (ella) conozca a Alfonso** (*I want her to meet Alfonso*)

A Espero que Sofía venga a la fiesta de mañana. Quiero que conozca a Alfonso. ¿Crees tú que vendrá?

B No creo que venga. Está preparando un exámen.

Diálogo 2: **No creo que pueda** (*I don't think I'll be able to*)

A Espero que haga buen tiempo mañana. Enrique quiere que salgamos de excursión. ¿Vendrás con nosotros?

B No creo que pueda. Tengo muchísimo que hacer.

muchísimo *very much*

PRACTIQUE

A *Express hope.*

Ejemplo: ¿*Irá* Ana a la fiesta?

Espero que *vaya*.

1 ¿*Irán* tus padres a Granada?
2 ¿*Volverán* tus amigos?
3 ¿*Estará* allí Mercedes?
4 ¿*Comprenderá* Jorge?
5 ¿*Sabrá* él dónde está Luis?
6 ¿*Vendrán* Gloria y Manuel este viernes?

B *Express doubt.*

Ejemplo: ¿Crees que ella *nos encontrará?*

No creo que nos *encuentre*.

1 ¿Crees que José *saldrá?*
2 ¿Crees que ellos *nos verán?*
3 ¿Crees que Cristina *lo hará?*
4 ¿Crees que Gustavo *le dirá?*
5 ¿Crees que ellos *nos invitarán?*
6 ¿Crees que Dolores *se marchará?*

C *Express wishes and give indirect commands.*

Ejemplo: *Ven* a mi fiesta.

Quiero que *vengas* a mi fiesta.

1 *Vuelve* mañana.
2 *Habla* con ella.
3 *Ven* en el coche.
4 *Llámame* esta tarde.
5 *Hazlo*.
6 *Ponlo* aquí.

Verbs of emotion

Verbs which express some kind of emotion such as **sentir** (*to be sorry*) and **alegrarse** (*to be glad*) call for the use of the subjunctive in the subordinate clause.

Alicia está enferma. *Alicia is ill.*
Siento mucho que esté enferma. *I'm very sorry she's ill.*
Es una pena que esté enferma. *It's a pity she's ill.*
Maricarmen se casa. *Maricarmen is getting married.*
Me alegro que se case. *I'm glad she's getting married.*

Diálogo 1: **Me alegro de que vengáis** (*I'm glad you're coming*)
A Hola. Supongo que vendréis con nosotros mañana.
B Desde luego.
A Fantástico. Me alegro mucho de que vengáis. Saldremos a las 8.00. ¿Qué os parece?
B De acuerdo. A las 8.00 en punto estaremos aquí.

las 8.00 en punto *at 8 o'clock sharp*   **fantástico** *fantastic*
desde luego *of course*

PRACTIQUE
  Reply to each of these statements saying you are glad or sorry about what is stated.
Ejemplo: Pedro y Angélica *se casan.* (Me alegro . . .)
          Me alegro de que *se casen.*
Voy a España.   (Me alegro . . .)
Manuel *está* enfermo.   (Siento mucho . . .)
No *hay* habitaciones.   (Sentimos mucho . . .)
Está lloviendo.   (Es una pena . . .)
Hace sol.   (Me alegro . . .)
Elena *vuelve* mañana.   (Nos alegramos . . .)

2 Impersonal expressions

Impersonal expressions with the verb **ser**, such as **Es una pena qu**
esté enferma, generally require the use of the subjunctive, excep
when there is certainty.

> Es una pena (una lástima) que ella no esté aquí.   *It's a pity she*
> *not here.*
> Es posible que el coche no funcione.   *It's possible that the ca*
> *may not work.*
> Es mejor que se lo digas.   *You'd better tell him.*
> Es importante que les escribas.   *It's important that you shou*
> *write to them.*

3 Time clauses

Certain expressions of time, when the action has not yet taken place
require the use of the subjunctive.

> **Cuando vea** a Marta se lo diré.   *When I see Marta I will tell he*
> Lo terminaré **antes de que** tú **vuelvas**.   *I'll finish it before yo*
> *return.*
> Estaremos aquí **hasta que** ellos **se marchen**.   *We'll be here unt*
> *they leave.*

4 Perfect Subjunctive

When the verb in the subordinate clause refers to the past (e.g. *I hop*
he has arrived, I'm sorry you have been ill, I am glad they have go
married), we can no longer use the Present Subjunctive. Instead, w
use the Perfect Subjunctive. This is made up of the Presen
Subjunctive of **haber** plus a past participle which is invariable (fo
regular past participles see Unit 17, for irregular ones see Unit 21

haya
hayas	lleg**ado**	(llegar — *to arrive*)
haya	com**ido**	(comer — *to eat*)
hayamos	sub**ido**	(subir — *to go up*)
hayáis		
hayan		

Espero que Julio haya enviado la correspondencia.   *I hope Julio has sent the mail.*

No creo que Isabel lo haya sabido.   *I don't think Isabel has known (heard) about it.*

Siento que hayas estado enfermo.   *I'm sorry you have been ill.*

Me alegro de que hayas tenido éxito.   *I'm glad you have been successful.*

Diálogo 2: **Espero que hayan reparado el coche** (*I hope they have repaired the car*)

A   Espero que hayan reparado el coche. Lo necesito para esta noche.

B   No creo que lo hayan hecho todavía. Dijeron que estaría listo esta tarde.

A   Espero que sí.

espero que sí   *I hope so*

PRACTIQUE

B   *Respond to these statements as suggested using the Present Subjunctive.*

Ejemplo: Ha hecho mal tiempo. (Es una pena . . .)
          Es una pena que *haya hecho* mal tiempo.

1 *Hemos alquilado* la casa.   (Me alegro . . .)
2 *He aprendido* español.   (Nos alegramos . . .)
3 *He perdido* mi reloj.   (Sentimos mucho . . .)
4 La reunión *ha sido* un éxito.   (Me alegro . . .)
5 Isabel no *ha venido*.   (Es mejor . . .)
6 Mi coche *se ha estropeado*.   (Es una lástima . . .)

35 More about the Subjunctive

1 Subjunctive with other Indicative Tenses

So far in our study of the subjunctive the main clause has always been
in the Present Indicative.

Espero que él lo sepa.	*I hope he knows about it.*
No creo que la conozcas.	*I don't think you know her.*
Quiero que vuelvas.	*I want you to return.*
Siento que haya muerto.	*I'm sorry he's died.*
Es una pena que haya fracasado.	*It's a pity he's failed.*

Generally, if the main verb is in the Present Indicative, the dependent
or subordinate clause may be in the Present Subjunctive or the Perfect
Subjunctive, as shown in the examples above. If the main verb is in
the past: Preterite (see Unit 23), Imperfect (see Unit 24), Conditional
(see Unit 30), Pluperfect (see Unit 28), Conditional Perfect (see Unit
30), then the verb in the subordinate clause must be either in the
Imperfect or Pluperfect Subjunctive.

2 Imperfect Subjunctive—formation

The Imperfect Subjunctive can be formed in two ways. The first is
directly derived from the third person plural of the Preterite. Here are
some examples:

Infinitive	*Preterite (3rd person pl.)*	*Imperfect Subjunctive (1st/3rd person sing.)*
llegar	llegaron	lleg**ara**
beber	bebieron	beb**iera**
vivir	vivieron	viv**iera**
estar	estuvieron	estuv**iera**
decir	dijeron	dij**era**
ir/ser	fueron	fu**era**
poner	pusieron	pus**iera**

Note that verbs which are irregular in the Preterite are also irregular in the Imperfect Subjunctive.

Here is the Imperfect Subjunctive of three regular verbs representing each of the three conjugations: **llegar** (*to arrive*), **comer** (*to eat*), **escribir** (*to write*). Note that -**er** and -**ir** verbs share the same endings:

llegar	**comer**	**escribir**
lleg**ara**	com**iera**	escrib**iera**
lleg**aras**	com**ieras**	escrib**ieras**
lleg**ara**	com**iera**	escrib**iera**
lleg**áramos**	com**iéramos**	escrib**iéramos**
lleg**arais**	com**ierais**	escrib**ierais**
lleg**aran**	com**ieran**	escrib**ieran**

The Imperfect Subjunctive has an alternative set of endings which are more frequently used than the first. Again, -**er** and -**ir** verbs share the same endings:

lleg**ase**	com**iese**	escrib**iese**
lleg**ases**	com**ieses**	escrib**ieses**
lleg**ase**	com**iese**	escrib**iese**
lleg**ásemos**	com**iésemos**	escrib**iésemos**
lleg**aseis**	com**ieseis**	escrib**ieseis**
lleg**asen**	com**iesen**	escrib**iesen**

3 Imperfect Subjunctive—uses

The uses of the Imperfect Subjunctive are those of the Subjunctive as a whole (as seen in Units 33 and 34). It is used in the subordinate clause when the main verb is in the past. (See section **1**, above.)

No **creí** que Gloria **viniese** (o **viniera**). *I didn't think Gloria would come.*

Esperaba que ella **llegase** (o **llegara**). *I was hoping she would arrive.*

Me gustaría que lo **hicieses** (o **hicieras**). *I would like you to do it.*

El nos **había** pedido que le **ayudásemos** (o **ayudáramos**).   *He had asked us to help him.*

Yo le **habría dicho** que se **marchase** (o **marchara**).   *I would have told him to leave.*

The Imperfect Subjunctive is often found associated with a verb in the Conditional tense.

Sería mejor que les **escribieses (escribieras)**.   *You'd better write to them.*

Me gustaría que **me acompañases (acompañaras)**.   *I would like you to accompany me.*

Preferiría que **fuésemos (fuéramos)** a Mallorca.   *I would prefer us to go to Mallorca.*

Diálogo 1: **Me gustaría que vinieses** (*I'd like you to come*)

A   Hola Ignacio.
B   Hola.
A   Mira, me gustaría que vinieses a cenar con nosotros mañana. Espero que no tengas nada que hacer.
B   Encantado. Muchas gracias.
A   Te esperamos a las 8.30. ¿De acuerdo?
B   Sí, está bien.

encantado   *delighted*

PRACTIQUE

A   *Complete these sentences with the correct form of the Imperfect Subjunctive.*

Ejemplo: Me gustaría que (*nosotros ir*) al teatro.
                   Me gustaría que *fuésemos* al teatro.

1 Preferiría que (*tú venir*) pasado mañana.
2 Sería mejor que (*nosotros terminar*) pronto.
3 Juan esperaba que (*ellos comprender*).
4 Yo quería que (*vosotros saber*) la verdad.
5 Nos gustaría que (*ellos casarse*).
6 Sería mejor que (*tú practicar*) más.

4 Imperfect Subjunctive with Conditional clauses

The Imperfect Subjunctive is also used in sentences with si (*if*) followed by a statement which is not a fact (e.g. *If I had money I would buy it*). The verb which follows must be in the Conditional Indicative tense.

> **Si tuviese (tuviera)** dinero lo **compraría**.   *If I had money I would buy it.*
> **Si pudiese** (pudiera) **iría**.   *If I could I would go.*

Note: If the clause with **si** (*if*) carries a verb in the Present Indicative, the next verb normally goes in the Future Indicative, not the Subjunctive.

> **Si tengo** alguna dificultad te lo **diré**.   *If I have any difficulty I'll tell you about it.*
> **Si** el tren **está** lleno **será** difícil encontrar asiento.   *If the train is full it will be difficult to find a seat.*

Diálogo 2: **Si tuviese dinero . . .** (*If I had money*)

A   ¿Sabes que Raúl vende su coche?
B   Ya lo sé. Es un coche estupendo. Si tuviese suficiente dinero se lo compraría.
A   ¿Por qué no pides dinero al banco?
B   Sí, lo he pensado. Quizá lo haga.

quizá   *perhaps*
Note: **quizá** may be followed by Subjunctive or Indicative.

PRACTIQUE

B *Complete these sentences with the appropriate form of the Imperfect Subjunctive of the verb in brackets.*

1 Si yo la (*conocer*) te la presentaría.
2 Si nosotros (*saber*) dónde está se lo diríamos.
3 Si ellos (*estudiar*) más aprobarían sus exámenes.
4 Si yo (*tener*) tiempo te ayudaría.
5 Si ella (*querer*) nos casaríamos.
6 Si nosotros (*tener*) vacaciones iríamos a Canarias.

5   Pluperfect Subjunctive

If you want to express ideas such as *If I had seen her I would have told her, if it had rained we wouldn't have gone*, then another Subjunctive tense must be used. This is the Pluperfect Subjunctive, much less frequent than the Present and the Imperfect. It is formed with the Imperfect Subjunctive of **haber** plus a past participle (for regular past participles see Unit 17, for irregular ones see Unit 21).

hubiera o **hubiese**	
hubieras o **hubieses**	lleg**ado** (llegar)
hubiera o **hubiese**	beb**ido** (beber)
hubiéramos o **hubiésemos**	sub**ido** (subir)
hubierais o **hubieseis**	
hubieran o **hubiesen**	

> Si ella hubiese llegado la habría visto.   *If she had arrived I would have seen her.*
> Si yo no hubiese bebido no estaría enfermo.   *If I hadn't drunk I wouldn't be ill.*

The Conditional Perfect in this type of sentence may be substituted by the Pluperfect Subjunctive with exactly the same meaning. This is a common feature of colloquial speech. Compare these sentences:

> Si me hubiesen invitado yo **habría** ido.
> Si me hubiesen invitado yo **hubiera** ido.
> *If they had invited me I would have gone.*

Note that we have used **hubiesen** and then **hubiera** in order to avoid repetition of the same sound.

36 Special verbs

A number of Spanish verbs have special constructions and can have special meanings. Here is a list of the most important. Some of their uses have been illustrated with examples.

1 *acabar*

(*a*) *To finish.*

(*b*) Acabar de + *infinitive. To have just done something.*
Acabamos de empezar.   *We have just started.*

2 *andar*

(*a*) *To walk.*

(*b*) Andar + *gerund. To be doing something.*
Ando buscando el reloj.   *I'm looking for the watch.*

3 *conocer*

(*a*) *To know, to be acquainted with* (a person or a place).
Conozco a Carmen.   *I know Carmen.*
Conozco Madrid.   *I know Madrid.*

(*b*) *To meet* (for the first time).
La conocí en Sevilla.   *I met her in Seville.*

(*c*) Conocerse.   *To meet.*
Nos conocimos en Córdoba.   *We met in Córdoba.*
Se conocieron en NuevaYork.   *They met in New York.*

4 *dar*

(*a*) *To give.*

(*b*) Dar igual/dar lo mismo. *To be all the same.*
Me da igual/lo mismo.   *It's all the same to me.*

(*c*) Dar un paseo/una vuelta. *To go for a walk.*
Dimos un paseo/una vuelta por el río.   *We went for a walk along the river.*

5 *estar*

(a)   Estar bien/mal. *To be well/unwell.*
(b)   Estar acostado. *To be in bed.*
(c)   Estar convencido. *To be convinced.*
(d)   Estar de acuerdo (con). *To be in agreement (with).*
(e)   Estar dispuesto. *To be willing.*
(f)   Estar escrito. *To be written.*
(g)   Estar listo. *To be ready.*
(h)   Estar muerto. *To be dead.*
(i)   Estar preocupado. *To be worried.*
(j)   Estar seguro. *To be sure.*
(k)   Estar sentado. *To be sitting.*
(For other uses of **Estar** see Units 3, 12, 20, 21.)

6 *hacer*

(a)   Hacer el favor de + infinitive.
      Haga el favor de venir. *Please come. Will you come?*
(b)   Hacer falta (+ infinitive). *To be necessary (+ inf.)*
      No hace falta decirle. *It's not necessary to tell him.*
(c)   Hacerle caso (a alguien). *To pay attention (to somebody).*
      No le hagas caso a ella. *Don't pay attention to her.*
(d)   Hacer una pregunta. *To ask a question.*
(e)   *With expressions of weather such as*
      Hace frío/calor/viento. *It's cold/hot/windy.*
(f)   *With expressions of time to indicate for.*
      ¿Cuánto tiempo hace que trabajas aquí? *For how long have you worked here?*
      Hace un año que trabajo aquí. *I have worked here for a year.*
(g)   *With expressions of time to indicate ago (with a verb in the past).*
      ¿Cuánto tiempo hace que llegaste? *How long ago did you arrive?*
      Llegué hace dos días. *I arrived two days ago.*

7 *llevar*

(a)   *To take (it implies movement).*
      Llevé a mis hijos de vacaciones. *I took my children on holiday.*
      Llevaré el coche al garaje. *I'll take the car to the garage.*
(b)   *To wear clothes.*
      Lleva una chaqueta azul. *He's wearing a blue jacket.*

(c)   Llevarse bien/mal.   *To get on well/badly.*
Teresa y Marta se llevan muy bien.   *Teresa and Marta get on very well.*
(d)   Llevar + *time* + *gerund*. *To have been doing something.*
Llevo un año estudiando español.   *I have been studying Spanish for a year.*
¿Cuánto tiempo llevas trabajando aquí?   *How long have you been working here?*
Note: The verb **vivir** is usually omitted in this context.
Llevo un año en Madrid.   *I've been (living) in Madrid for a year.*

8 *ponerse*

(a)   *To put on clothes.*
Se puso la chaqueta.   *He put on his jacket.*
(b)   *To become (condition or state).*
Ella se puso triste.   *She became sad.*
Me puse enfermo.   *I became ill.*
(c)   *To begin to do something.*
Me puse a trabajar.   *I began to work.*
Se puso a llover.   *It began to rain.*

9 *quedar*

(a)   *To be left/to have left.*
¿Cuánto dinero te queda?   *How much have you got left?*
Me quedan 1.000 pesetas.   *I have 1,000 pesetas left.*
(b)   Quedar (en).   *To agree.*
Quedamos en vernos.   *We agreed to see each other.*
Quedamos a las 4.00.   *We agreed to meet at 4.00.*
(c)   Quedarse.   *To stay.*
Voy a quedarme dos días.   *I'm going to stay two days.*

10 *ser*

(a)   Ser aficionado a. *To be fond of.*
(b)   Ser agradable. *To be pleasant.*
(c)   Ser amable. *To be kind.*
(d)   Ser capaz/incapaz. *To be capable/incapable.*
(e)   Ser cierto/verdad. *To be true.*
(f)   Ser muy amigos. *To be good friends.*
(g)   Ser necesario. *To be necessary.*

(*h*)   Ser posible/imposible. *To be possible/impossible.*
(*i*)   Ser suficiente. *To be sufficient.*
(For other uses of **Ser** see Units 3, 5, 13, 17 and 25.)

11   *tener*

(*a*)   Tener años. *To be years old.*
  ¿Cuántos años tienes?   *How old are you?*
  Tengo 25 años.   *I'm 25 years old.*
(*b*)   Tener calor/frío. *To be hot/cold.*
(*c*)   Tener una cita. *To have an appointment.*
(*d*)   Tener cuidado. *To be careful.*
(*e*)   Tener dolor. *To have a pain.*
(*f*)   Tener éxito. *To be successful.*
(*g*)   Tener hambre/sed. *To be hungry/thirsty.*
(*h*)   Tener hora. *To have the time.*
  ¿Tienes hora? *Have you got the time?*
(*i*)   Tener miedo. *To be afraid.*
(*j*)   Tener razón. *To be right.*
(*k*)   Tener sueño. *To be sleepy.*
(For other uses of **Tener** see Units 8, 18, 31 and 32.)

12   *volver*

(*a*)   *To return*
(*b*)   Volver a + *infinitive. To do something again.*
  Volveré a hacerlo.   *I'll do it again.*
  Volvió a equivocarse.   *He made a mistake again.*

37 Prepositions

Prepositions are words such as **a, de, en, por, para**. Throughout this book you have learned a number of prepositions in context. Here are some examples of prepositions you should be familiar with.

Llega **a** Madrid a las 3.00.   *It arrives in Madrid at 3.00.*
Sale **de** Londres a las 12.00.   *It leaves London at 12.00.*
Soy **de** San Francisco.   *I am from San Francisco.*
Vive **en** Nueva York.   *He lives in New York.*
Dimos un paseo **por** el río.   *We went for a walk along the river.*
Su mujer le espera **para** merendar.   *His wife is waiting for him to have a snack.*

The following list contains the main Spanish prepositions with examples.

1   *a*   (*to, in, on, at*)

Vamos **a** Mallorca.	*We're going to Mallorca.*
Llegaron **a** Palma.	*They arrived in Palma.*
Está **a** la derecha.	*It's on the right.*
Se sentó **a** la mesa.	*He sat at the table.*
¿ **A** qué hora?	*At what time?*

A is sometimes not translated into English.

A mí me gusta.	*I like it.* (emphatic)
Conozco **a** Luis.	*I know Luis.* (personal '**a**')

A + **el** becomes **al**.

Voy **al** cine.   *I'm going to the cinema.*

Al may translate also as *on*.

Al salir la vi.   *On going out I saw her.*

2   *con*   (*with*)

Iré **con** Francisca.	*I'll go with Francisca.*
Iremos **con** ellos.	*We'll go with them.*

Note the forms **conmigo** (*with me*) and **contigo** (*with you*, familiar) which are exceptions.

¿Vendrás conmigo?	*Will you come with me?*
Sí, iré contigo.	*Yes, I'll go with you.*

3   *de* (*of, from, by, in, about*)

Una botella **de** vino.	*A bottle of wine.*
Ella es **de** Gerona.	*She's from Gerona.*
Trabaja **de** día/noche.	*He works by day/night.*
Las 4.00 **de** la tarde.	*4 o'clock in the afternoon.*
Hablaban **de** Juan.	*They were talking about Juan.*

De is sometimes not translated into English.

Una maleta **de** cuero.	*A leather suitcase.*
Una cuchara **de** madera.	*A wooden spoon.*
¿**De** quién es?	*Whose is it?*
Es **del** señor García.	*It's señor García's.*

Note that **de + el** becomes **del**.

There are many phrases and expressions in Spanish which contain the preposition **de**.

La sala **de** estar.	*Sitting-room.*
El cuarto **de** baño.	*Bathroom.*
La agencia **de** viajes.	*Travel agency.*
El fin **de** semana.	*Weekend.*
El cepillo **de** dientes.	*Toothbrush.*

4   *desde* (*from, since*)

Desde Londres a Madrid.	*From London to Madrid.*
Desde las 5.30.	*Since 5.30.*

5.   *en* (*in, on, at, by, about*)

Están **en** Santander.	*They're in Santander.*
Está **en** la mesa.	*It's on the table.*
Está **en** la esquina.	*It's at the corner.*
Fuimos **en** tren.	*We went by train.*
Pienso mucho **en** él.	*I think a lot about him.*

6   *entre* (*between, among*)

La farmacia está **entre** el banco y Correos.	*The chemist's is between the bank and the post-office.*
Entre ellos estaba Ana Luisa.	*Ana Luisa was among them.*

7 *hacia* (*towards, about*)

Ibamos **hacia** la oficina.	*We were going towards the office.*
Ocurrió **hacia** las 2.00.	*It happened about 2.00.*

8 *hasta* (*until, as far as*)

Trabajé **hasta** muy tarde.	*I worked until very late.*
Hasta mañana.	*See you tomorrow (until tomorrow).*
Hasta luego.	*See you later.*
La acompañé **hasta** casa.	*I accompanied her as far as her house.*

9 *para* (*for, in order to, towards, to*)

Este pastel es **para** ti.	*This cake is for you.*
Es difícil **para** mí.	*It's difficult for me.*
Voy a España **para** practicar mi español.	*I'm going to Spain in order to practise my Spanish.*
Iba **para** la estación.	*I was going towards (to) the station.*

10 *por* (*for, by, because of, through, along, in*)

Lo hizo **por** el dinero.	*He did it for the money.*
Viajó **por** un año.	*He travelled for a year.*
Viajaron **por** barco.	*They travelled by boat.*
Por la lluvia no fuimos.	*Because of the rain we didn't go.*
Entré **por** la puerta principal.	*I came in through the main door.*
Andaba **por** la calle.	*He was walking along the street.*
Llegaron **por** la tarde.	*They arrived in the afternoon.*

There are many expressions which contain the preposition **por**.

¿**Por** cuánto tiempo?	*For how long?*
Por eso.	*That's why.*
Por favor.	*Please.*
Por fin.	*At last.*
Por lo general.	*Generally.*
Por semana/mes/año.	*Per week/month/year.*
¿**Por** qué?	*Why?*
Por una parte.	*On the one hand.*
Por otra parte.	*On the other hand.*
Por (lo) tanto.	*Therefore.*
Por último.	*Finally.*

11 *sin* (*without*)

Estábamos **sin** dinero.	*We were without money.*
No iremos **sin** ti.	*We won't go without you.*
Lo hice **sin** pensar.	*I did it without thinking.*

12   *sobre* (*about, on, over*)

Vimos una película **sobre** España.   *We saw a film about Spain.*
El libro está **sobre** la mesa.   *The book is on the table.*
El cuadro está en la pared **sobre** el sillón.   *The picture is on the wall above the armchair.*

The following are some common compound Spanish prepositions.

1   *además de* (*in addition to, besides*)

Hablo español **además de** francés.   *I speak Spanish in addition to French.*

2   *alrededor de* (*around*)

Llegaron **alrededor de** la 1.00.   *They arrived around 1.00.*

3   *antes de* (*before*)

Teresa telefoneó a Lola **antes de** salir.   *Teresa telephoned Lola before going out.*

4   *cerca de* (*near*)

Viven **cerca de** aquí.   *They live near here.*

5   *debajo de* (*underneath*)

La pelota está **debajo de** la mesa.   *The ball is underneath the table.*

6   *después de* (*after*)

Después de cenar iremos al cine.   *After dinner we'll go to the cinema.*

7   *detrás de* (*behind*)

El mercado está **detrás de** la iglesia.   *The market is behind the church.*

8   *fuera de* (*outside*)

Carlos está **fuera de** la casa.   *Carlos is outside the house.*

9   *lejos de* (*far from*)

El parque está **lejos de** aquí.   *The park is far from here.*

Key to the Exercises

Unidad 3

A 1 es 2 es 3 somos 4 son 5 es 6 Es
C 1 está 2 está 3 están 4 estan 5 estáis 6 estamos
D soy/es/soy/está/estoy
E Me llamo (*your name*). Soy (*your nationality*). Soy de (*place of origin*). Estoy (*single or married*).

Unidad 4

A 1 No, no es español. Es mexicano. 2 No, no es bueno. Es malo. 3 No, no está en Barcelona. Está en Bilbao. 4 No, no estoy casado. Estoy soltero. 5 No, no son buenos. Son malos. 6 No, no están en España. Están en Venezuela.
B 1 ¿Está en Segovia Paco? 2 ¿Son de Córdoba Paloma y Rocío? 3 ¿Es bueno el Camping El Sol? 4 ¿Es bonito Toledo? 5 ¿Está bien Pepe? 6 ¿Están solteros Ricardo y Cristóbal?
C 1 ¿De dónde? 2 ¿Cuánto es? 3 ¿Dónde? 4 ¿Cómo? 5 ¿Quién? 6 ¿Quiénes?

Unidad 5

A El Hotel Victoria es un hotel de una estrella. Es muy pequeño. Las habitaciones son oscuras. La comida es regular. El servicio es bastante malo.
B Me llamo Julia. Soy una chica alta y delgada. Soy bonita y simpática.

C 1 son 2 es 3 sois 4 somos 5 es 6 son
D Hace bastante frío pero hace sol. ¿Qué tiempo hace allí?

Unidad 6

A 1 Este 2 Estos 3 Este 4 Estas 5 esta 6 Estas
B 1 ¿Cuánto cuesta ese vestido? 2 ¿Cuánto cuestan esos pantalones? 3 ¿Cuánto cuesta esa camisa? 4 ¿Cuánto cuestan esos zapatos? 5 ¿Cuánto cuestan esas blusas? 6 ¿Cuánto cuesta ese traje?
C 1 éste o ése 2 éstos o ésos 3 éstas o ésas 4 ésta o ésa 5 éste o ése 6 ésta o ésa

Unidad 7

A 1 No, mi cámara es japonesa. 2 No, mis zapatos son negros. 3 No, mi radio es grande. 4 No, mi coche es un Seat. 5 No, mis pantalones son marrones. 6 No, mis postales son de Madrid.
B No, nuestros hijos están en Inglaterra. Estoy aquí con mi marido/mujer. ¿Están aquí sus hijos?/¿De dónde son ustedes?/ Nuestra casa está en Londres.
C 1 Es el coche del Sr Pérez. 2 Es la habitación de Carlos. 3 Son los zapatos de mi hija. 4 Es la chaqueta de Laura. 5 Son los pantalones de Jorge. 6 Es el chico de la Sra Ramírez.
D 1 La mía es marrón. 2 El mío es inglés. 3 Los míos son franceses. 4 El

mío es aquél. 5 La mía es grande.
6 Los míos son de Cataluña.

E 1 las nuestras 2 suyo 3 vuestros 4
la tuya 5 vuestra 6 nuestra

Unidad 8

A 1 tienes 2 tengo 3 tenemos 4 tiene
5 tenéis 6 Tiene
B 1 ¿Tiene Vd. una habitación
individual? 2 ¿Tiene Vd. una mesa
para dos? 3 ¿Tiene Vd. periódicos
ingleses? 4 ¿Tiene Vd. cambio?
5 ¿Tiene Vd. la cuenta? 6 ¿Tiene Vd.
mi billete?
C 1 tenéis 2 tengo 3 Tienes
4 tenemos 5 tiene 6 tienen
D 1 Tengo pasaporte (británico/
americano). 2 Tengo (*your age*)
años. 3 Tengo (2/3) hermanos.
Tengo (2/3 hijos). No tengo
hermanos/hijos. 4 Tengo una
casa/un piso. 5 Tiene (2/3)
habitaciones.

Unidad 9

A *Ejemplo:* A ¿Cuánto cuestan
estas manzanas?/B Setenta pesetas
el kilo./A ¿Y aquéllas?/B Aquéllas son más caras, pero son
mejores que éstas. Cuestan noventa
pesetas.
B 1 El Club Montserrat es el más
confortable. 2 La Pensión Bellavista
es la más barata. 3 El Bar Paco y el
Bar Gustavo son los más tranquilos.
4 El Restaurante Gracia es el más
agradable. 5 La Cafetería Roma y la
Cafetería Rosa son las más grandes.
6 El Café Los Artistas es el más
antiguo.
C 1 tantos . . . como 2 tanto . . .
como 3 tanto . . . como 4 tantos . . .
como 5 tantas . . . como 6
tantas . . . como

Unidad 10

A *Ejemplo:* A Buenos días
(Buenas tardes). ¿Hay una farmacia
por aquí?/B Sí, hay una en la
plaza./A Muchas gracias./B De
nada.
B 1 Sí, hay dos. 2 Sí, hay una. 3 Sí,
hay televisión. 4 No, no hay
teléfono. 5 No, no hay
aparcamiento.
C B Sí, había quince personas./
Sí, había dos amigos míos, Alberto y
Marisol./Sí, había mucha comida.

Unidad 11

A 1 No hay nada. 2 No tengo nada
que declarar. 3 No tengo nada. 4 No
hay nadie. 5 No hay ninguno. 6 No
hay ninguna.
B 1 ningún 2 alguna 3 nada
4 alguien 5 Algo 6 nadie
C 1 No, no tengo otros. 2 No, no
tengo otra. 3 No, no tengo otras.
4 No, no tengo otro.
D 1 toda 2 Todos 3 todo 4 Todas

Unidad 12

A 1 ¿Dónde está la estación de
autobuses? Está enfrente de correos.
2 ¿Dónde está la estación de
servicio? Está al lado del hospital. 3
¿Dónde están los servicios? Están
detrás del ayuntamiento. 4 ¿Dónde
está el garaje? Está junto a la
estación de servicio. 5 ¿Dónde está la
catedral? Está en la plaza. 6 ¿Dónde
está el museo? Está cerca de la
catedral.
B 1 Bilbao está en el norte de
España. 2 Sitges está a 35 kilómetros
de Barcelona. 3 Valencia está en el
este de España. 4 Las Islas Baleares
están en el Mediterráneo. 5

Fuengirola está a una hora de Málaga. 6 El ayuntamiento está a tres calles de aquí.
C 1 Mi casa/piso está en (*name of town*). 2 Está en (*part of town*). 3 Está en (*country or town*).

Unidad 13

A 1 ¿Qué hora es? o ¿Tiene hora? Es la una y diez. 2 Es la una y veinte. 3 Son las cuatro y media. 4 Son las cinco. 5 Son las siete menos veinte. 6 Son las siete y cuarto. 7 Son las diez menos diez. 8 Son las diez y diez. 9 Son las doce menos cuarto.
B 1 Es a las ocho. 2 Es a las once menos cuarto. 3 Es a las nueve y cuarto. 4 Es a las ocho y media.

Unidad 14

A 1 viajan 2 estudiáis 3 hablas 4 abre 5 comprendo. 6 recibe
B 1 Yo también llego a las 9.00. 2 Yo también desayuno a las 8.00. 3 Yo también viajo mucho. 4 Yo también bebo cerveza. 5 Yo también respondo todas mis cartas. 6 Yo también recibo muchos amigos en casa.
C 1 Yo tampoco respondo mis cartas. 2 Yo tampoco escribo mucho. 3 Yo tampoco bebo vino. 4 Yo tampoco viajo a Sudamérica. 5 Yo tampoco hablo alemán. 6 Yo tampoco desayuno.
D 1 Trabajo/estudio. 2 Trabajo/ estudio en (*name of the place where you work or study*). 3 Vivo en (*town or part of town where you live*). 4 Vivo con mi familia/con amigos/solo(a). 5 Hablo inglés/francés/alemán/un poco de español, etc. 6 Sí, viajo a España/No viajo a España. 7 Viajo a Mallorca/a París, etc.

Unidad 15

A 1 te 2 me 3 se 4 os 5 Nos 6 se
B 1 se afeita 2 te levantas 3 me baño 4 se halla 5 nos olvidamos 6 se ve
C 1 Me levanto a las (*time*). 2 Me marcho a las (*time*). 3 Me acuesto a las (*time*).

Unidad 16

A 1 conozco/salgo 2 va 3 hago 4 sale/salgo 5 vamos 6 sé
B 1 cojo 2 doy 3 Conozco 4 Pertenezco 5 Vengo 6 Traigo
C 1 entiende 2 entiendo 3 empieza 4 viene 5 recuerdo 6 vuelven
·D 1 Sí, conozco España. Conozco Madrid. (No conozco España.) 2 Conozco España, Francia, Italia, etc. 3 Sí, entiendo el español/el francés. (No entiendo el español/el francés.) 4 Sí voy al extranjero. Voy a España. (No voy al extranjero.) 5 Juego al tenis/fútbol, etc.

Unidad 17

A 1 En Inglaterra se bebe mucho té. 2 En Andalucía se come mucho pescado. 3 En Chile se habla español. 4 En España se da mucha importancia a las fiestas. 5 En Brasil se habla portugués. 6 En Inglaterra se conduce por la izquierda.
B 1 El pan se compra en la panadería. 2 La fruta y las verduras se venden en el mercado. 3 La gasolina se vende en la estación de servicio. 4 Los cheques de viajero se cambian en el banco. 5 Las cartas se echan en correos. 6 Los seguros se obtienen en la agencia de viajes.
C 1 Se piensa que es posible. 2 Se cree que está en Marbella. 3 ¿A qué

hora se sale de Madrid? 4 ¿A qué hora se llega a Toledo? 5 ¿Qué carretera se toma para ir a Avila? 6 ¿Dónde se coge el autobús?

Unidad 18

A 1 Voy a comprar una camisa. 2 Voy a cenar en casa. 3 Voy a volver a las 8.00. 4 Voy a viajar en octubre. 5 No voy a hacer nada. 6 Voy a escoger el negro.

B 1 Tengo que 2 Quieren 3 Prefiere 4 No pueden 5 Acaba de 6 Debo

Unidad 19

A 1 les (o los) 2 la 3 lo 4 la 5 Les (o Los) 6 La

B 1 Ahora se la doy. 2 Ahora se lo digo. 3 Ahora se la paso. 4 Ahora se lo paso. 5 Ahora se las cambio. 6 Ahora se la doy.

Unidad 20

A 1 Está desayunando. 2 Estamos estudiando. 3 Están jugando. 4 Estoy leyendo. 5 Estamos comiendo. 6 Estoy tomando el sol.

B 1 Estoy escribiéndola. 2 Estoy escribiéndoles. 3 Estoy respondiéndole. 4 Estoy lavándola. 5 Estoy limpiándolo. 6 Estoy sirviéndola.

Unidad 21

1 La farmacia está abierta. 2 Estos platos están rotos. 3 Todo está dicho. 4 Las reservas están hechas. 5 El problema está terminado. 6 El examen está corregido.

Unidad 22

A 1 (No) me gusta el verano. 2 (No) me gusta el invierno. 3 (No) me gusta la primavera. 4 (No) me gusta el otoño. 5 (No) me gustan las flores. 6 (No) me gustan las Navidades.

B 1 ¿Te gusta el curso? 2 ¿Te gustan los profesores? 3 ¿Te gusta la universidad? 4 ¿Te gustan los estudiantes? 5 ¿Te gusta aprender español? 6 ¿Te gusta enseñar?

C 1 El tiempo me parece estupendo. 2 Las playas me parecen excelentes. 3 La comida me parece muy buena. 4 Los camareros me parecen agradables. 5 La habitación me parece muy calurosa. 6 El servicio me parece regular.

Unidad 23

A 1 estudió 2 viajé 3 volvieron 4 pasaste 5 vivieron 6 vendimos

B 1 Se levantó a las 7.00. 2 Tomó un café con leche. 3 Salió de casa a las 8.30. 4 Cogió el autobús. 5 Comenzó a trabajar a las 9.00. 6 Comió a la 1.00 en una cafetería. 7 A las 2.00 volvió al trabajo. 8 Terminó a las 5.00. 9 Volvió a casa. 10 Escuchó la radio, escribió una carta, descansó un momento y a las 8.30 cenó. 11 Se acostó a las 11.00.

C 1 anduvimos 2 tuve que 3 puso 4 dio 5 dijo 6 hicieron

D 1 Las pasé en (*country or town*). 2 Fui con (*the person or people with whom you went*). 3 Estuve (*number of days or weeks*) días/semanas. 4 Tomé el sol, me bañé, salí de excursión, dormí mucho, etc. 5 Sí, me gustó (mucho)/No me gustó. 6 Volví el (*date, e.g.* 15 de julio).

Unidad 24

desayunaba / salía / Cogía /llegaba /
leía /empezaba / hablaba / dejaba /
iba / trabajaba / se ponía / volvía /
esperaba / leía / veía.

Unidad 25

A 1 Estaba en Palma de Mallorca.
2 Tenía cuatro habitaciones. 3 Tenía
dos cuartos de baño. 4 La terraza era
muy grande. 5 Estaba a cien metros
de la playa. 6 Costaba cuatro
millones de pesetas.
B salí / Eran / estaba / Había /
Bebí / fumé / escuchaba / llamó /
Eran.

Unidad 26

1 que 2 la cual 3 donde 4 quien 5 el ·
cual 6 quienes

Unidad 27

A 1 Sí, ya la he preparado. 2 No,
todavía no la he recibido. 3 No,
todavía no la he limpiado. 4 Sí, ya los
hemos reservado. 5 No, todavía no
lo han escuchado. 6 Sí, ya las hemos
encontrado.
B 1 he escrito 2 ha abierto 3 hemos
visto 4 ha muerto 5 he dicho 6 has
hecho

Unidad 28

1 había salido 2 había empezado 3 se
había marchado 4 habían vuelto 5 te
habías acostado. 6 había parado

Unidad 29

A llegaré/iré/cogeré/estaré/llevaré/
me quedaré

B 1 No, pero la haré pronto. 2 No,
pero lo obtendré pasado mañana. 3
No, pero se lo diré esta noche. 4 No,
pero la pondré ahora. 5 No, pero me
la pondré el domingo. 6 No, pero las
haré por la mañana.

Unidad 30

A 1 Mi padre dijo que compraría
aquel coche. 2 . . . que alquilarían el
piso. 3 . . . que se marcharía pronto.
4 . . . que se levantarían a las 7.00.
5 . . . que pasarías un mes en
San Francisco. 6 . . . que les
acompañaría.
B 1 haría 2 podrías 3 saldrían
4 diría 5 tendrían que 6 vendría
C 1 Yo lo habría hecho. 2 Yo se lo
habría dicho. 3 Yo la habría
invitado. 4 Yo se lo habría dado.
5 Yo les habría escrito. 6 Yo lo
habría leído.

Unidad 31

A 1 tienes que 2 Tendré que
3 Tuvimos que 4 Tendréis que 5
tuvieron que 6 Tuvo que
B 1 Tuvimos que esperar dos
horas. 2 Tendrán que volver
mañana. 3 No debería comer pan.
4 Hay que estudiar. 4 ¿Es necesario
reservar una mesa? (o ¿Hay que
reservar una mesa?) 6 Necesito verla.

Unidad 32

A 1 Doble 2 Siga 3 Cruce 4 Tome
5 Ceda 6 Haga
B 1 Traiga su pasaporte. 2 Vengan
mañana. 3 Vaya a Correos y
cómpreme cinco sellos . . . 4
Telefonée y reserve la habitación.
5 No fumen. 6 Vuelvan a las 5.00.

C coge / coge / bájate / dobla / sigue / dobla / cruza

Unidad 33

A 1 Espero que vayan. 2 Espero que vuelvan. 3 Espero que esté. 4 Espero que comprenda. 5 Espero que lo sepa. 6 Espero que vengan.
B 1 No creo que salga. 2 No creo que nos vean. 3 No creo que lo haga. 4 No creo que le diga. 5 No creo que nos inviten. 6 No creo que se marche.
C 1 Quiero que vuelvas mañana. 2 Quiero que hables con ella. 3 Quiero que vengas en el coche. 4 Quiero que me llames esta tarde. 5 Quiero que lo hagas. 6 Quiero que lo pongas aquí.

Unidad 34

A 1 Me alegro de que vaya(s). 2 Siento mucho que esté enfermo. 3 Sentimos mucho que no haya_ habitaciones. 4 Es una pena que esté lloviendo. 5 Me alegro de que haga sol. 6 Nos alegramos de que vuelva mañana.
B 1 Me alegro de que hayan (o hayáis) alquilado la casa. 2 Nos alegramos de que haya (o hayas) aprendido español. 3 Sentimos mucho que haya (o hayas) perdido su (tu) reloj. 4 Me alegro de que la reunión haya sido un éxito. 5 Es mejor que Isabel no haya venido. 6 Es una lástima que su (o tu) coche se haya estropeado.

Unidad 35

A 1 vinieses 2 terminásemos 3 comprendiesen 4 supieseis 5 se casasen 6 practicases
B 1 conociera o conociese 2 supiéramos o supiésemos 3 estudiaran o estudiasen 4 tuviera o tuviese 5 quisiera o quisiese 6 tuviéramos o tuviésemos

Appendix 1

Los números (*Numbers*)

0	cero	7	siete	14	catorce
1	uno	8	ocho	15	quince
2	dos	9	nueve	16	dieciséis
3	tres	10	diez	17	diecisiete
4	cuatro	11	once	18	dieciocho
5	cinco	12	doce	19	diecinueve
6	seis	13	trece	20	veinte

efore a masculine noun **uno** becomes **un** and before a feminine noun **una**: **un** ñor (*one gentleman*), **una** señora (*one lady*).

21	veintiuno	26	veintiséis
22	veintidós	27	veintisiete
23	veintitrés	28	veintiocho
24	veinticuatro	29	veintinueve
25	veinticinco	30	treinta
31	treinta y uno	36	treinta y seis
32	treinta y dos	37	treinta y siete
33	treinta y tres	38	treinta y ocho
34	treinta y cuatro	39	treinta y nueve
35	treinta y cinco	40	cuarenta

ll numbers finishing in **uno**, e.g. **veintiuno, treinta y uno**, change as **uno** ove: el día — veinti**ún** días; la semana — veinti**una** semanas.

41	cuarenta y uno	70	setenta
42	cuarenta y dos	80	ochenta
43	cuarenta y tres	90	noventa
44	cuarenta y cuatro	100	cien
		101	ciento uno
50	cincuenta	102	ciento dos
51	cincuenta y uno		
52	cincuenta y dos	201	doscientos uno
		202	doscientos dos
60	sesenta	300	trescientos

Numbers which finish in **-cientos**, e.g. **doscientos, trescientos**, must change according to the gender of the noun which follows: el dólar — **doscientos** dólares; la peseta — **doscientas** pesetas. Note that **cien** (*one hundred*) does not change: cien dólares (*one hundred dollars*); cien pesetas (*one hundred pesetas*).

400	cuatrocientos	1000	mil
500	quinientos	1001	mil uno
600	seiscientos	1500	mil quinientos
700	setecientos	2000	dos mil
800	ochocientos	1.000.000	un millón
900	novecientos	2.000.000	dos millones

Note that **millón** forms the plural by adding **-es** and losing the accent. After **millions** or **millones** we must use the preposition **de**. Compare these phrases

Mil personas.   *One thousand people.*
Dos mil personas.   *Two thousand people.*
Un millón **de** personas.   *One millon people.*
Dos millones **de** personas.   *Two million people.*

Look at the way dates are read in Spanish.
1980   mil novecientos ochenta.
1987   mil novecientos ochenta y siete.

Los números ordinales (*Ordinal numbers*)

primero	*first*	sexto	*sixth*
segundo	*second*	séptimo	*seventh*
tercero	*third*	octavo	*eighth*
cuarto	*fourth*	noveno	*nineth*
quinto	*fifth*	décimo	*tenth*

Ordinal numbers have masculine and feminine forms.
El segundo año.   *The second year.*
La segunda semana.   *The second week.*

Primero and **tercero** drop the **-o** before a masculine noun.
El primer piso.   *The first floor.*
El tercer día.   *The third day.*

Los días de la semana (*The days of the week*)

lunes	*Monday*	viernes	*Friday*
martes	*Tuesday*	sábado	*Saturday*
miércoles	*Wednesday*	domingo	*Sunday*
jueves	*Thursday*		

Note:
el sábado   *on Saturday*
los sábados   *Saturdays*

todos los domingos   *every Sunday*
el miércoles 24   *on Monday 24th*

Los meses del año (*The months of the year*)

enero	*January*	julio	*July*
febrero	*February*	agosto	*August*
marzo	*March*	se(p)tiembre	*September*
abril	*April*	octubre	*October*
mayo	*May*	noviembre	*November*
junio	*June*	diciembre	*December*

Note: en julio   *in July*
el 4 de julio   *on 4th July*
el 21 de abril de 1988   *on 21st April 1988*

Las estaciones del año (*The seasons*)

el invierno   *winter*
el otoño   *autumn*

la primavera   *spring*
el verano   *summer*

Los colores (*The colours*)

amarillo	*yellow*
azul	*blue*
blanco	*white*
gris	*grey*
marrón	*brown*
color naranja	*orange*
negro	*black*
rojo	*red*
verde	*green*

Note: To refer to colours in general we use **el** (*the*, masc.)
Me gusta el amarillo.   *I like yellow.*

But if colours refer to a specific noun they must agree with it in gender and number:
Me gusta la camisa blanca.   *I like the white shirt.*

Light and *dark* are **claro** and **oscuro** respectively.
verde claro   *light green*   marrón oscuro   *dark brown*

Appendix 2: Table of Common Irregular Verbs

All tenses are not given, but by remembering the following simple rules the student can easily form any tense from the parts of the verb that are shown:

1. The stem of the Imperfect Indicative is regular, except in the cases of **ir (iba), ver (veía)** and **ser (era)**. See Unit 24.
2. The Conditional, like the Future tense, is formed from the whole infinitive, but with the endings of the Imperfect tense of **-er** and **-ir** verbs: **ía, -ías, -ía, -íamos, -íais, -ían**. See Units 29 and 30.
3. With the exception of **saber (sepa), haber (haya), dar (dé), ser (sea), ir (vaya)**, the stem of the Present Subjunctive is the same as that of the first person singular of the Present Indicative. The first and third person singular of the Present Subjunctive correspond in form to formal commands. See Units 32 and 33.
4. The Imperfect Subjunctive tense can be formed from the third person plural of the Preterite. See Units 23 and 35.

Verbs whose irregularities depend only on orthographic or stem-changing peculiarities are not included in this table. See Unit 16.

Compounds have also been omitted. For **mantener, proponer**, see the simple verbs **tener, poner**, etc.

Infinitive	Pres. Ind	Preterite	Future	Participles
andar *to go, walk*	ando	anduve	andaré	andando
	—	—		andado
caber *to be contained in*	quepo	cupe	cabré	cabiendo
	cabe	—	—	cabido
	cabemos	—	—	—
	caben	—	—	—
caer *to fall*	caigo	caí	caeré	cayendo
	cae	cayó	—	caído
		caímos	—	—
	caen	cayeron	—	—
conducir *to drive*	conduzco	conduje	conduciré	conduciendo
	conduce	condujo	—	conducido
		condujeron		
dar *to give*	doy	di	daré	dando
	da	dió	—	dado
decir *to say, tell*	digo	dije	diré	diciendo
	dice	dijo	—	dicho
	decimos	dijimos	—	—
	dicen	dijeron	—	—
estar *to be*	estoy	estuve	estare	estando
	está	—		estado
	están			
haber *to have*	he	hube	habre	habiendo
	ha	hubo	—	habido
	hemos	hubimos	—	—
	han	hubieron	—	—

Infinitive	Pres. Ind	Preterite	Future	Participles
hacer *to do, make*	hago	hice	haré	haciendo
	hace	hizo		hecho
	—	hicimos		—
ir *to go*	hacen	—		—
	voy	fui	iré	yendo
	va	fue		ido
	—	fuimos		—
oir *to hear*	van	fueron		—
	oigo	oí	oiré	oyendo
	oye	oyó		oído
	oímos	oímos		—
	oyen	oyeron		—
poder *to be able*	puedo	pude	podré	pudiendo
	podemos	pudimos		podido
	pueden	pudieron		—
poner *to put*	pongo	puse	pondré	poniendo
	pone			puesto
	—	pusimos		—
	ponen	pusieron		—
querer *to want, love*	quiero	quise	querré	queriendo
	queremos	quisimos		querido
	quieren	quisieron		—
reir *to laugh*	río	reí	reiré	riendo
	—	rió		reído
	reímos	reímos		—
	ríen	rieron		—

Infinitive	Present	Preterite	Future	Gerund / Past Participle
saber *to know*	sé	supe	sabré	sabiendo
	sabe	supimos	—	sabido
	saben	supieron		—
salir *to go out*	salgo	salí	saldré	saliendo
	sale	salió	—	salido
	salimos	salieron		—
ser *to be*	soy	fui	seré	siendo
	—	—	—	sido
	es	fue		—
	somos	—		—
	son	fueron		
tener *to have*	tengo	tuve	tendré	teniendo
	tiene	tuvo	—	tenido
	tenemos	tuvimos		—
	tienen	tuvieron		—
traer *to bring*	traigo	traje	traeré	trayendo
	trae	trajo	—	traído
	traemos	trajeron		—
valer *to be worth*	valgo	valí	valdré	valiendo
	vale	valió	—	valido
	valemos	valieron		—
venir *to come*	vengo	vine	vendré	viniendo
	viene	vino	—	venido
	venimos	vinimos		—
	vienen	vinieron		—
ver *to see*	veo	vi	veré	viendo
	ve	vió	—	visto
	vemos	vimos		—

Spanish – English Vocabulary

a   *to, in, on, at*
abajo   *downstairs*
abierto   *open*
abril   *April*
abrir   *to open*
absoluto: en —   *not at all*
abuelo (m)   *grandfather*
abuelos (m pl)   *grandparents*
acabar   *to finish*
acabar de + *infinitive*   *to have just* + *past part.*
aceite (m)   *oil*
acompañar   *to accompany*
acordarse   *to remember*
acostarse   *to go to bed*
acuerdo: de —   *all right*
además   *besides*
además de   *in addition to*
adiós   *goodbye*
¿adónde?   *where to?*
aduana (f)   *customs*
aeropuerto (m)   *airport*
afeitarse   *to shave*
aficionado: ser — a   *to be fond of*
agencia de viajes (f)   *travel agency*
agosto   *August*
agradable   *pleasant*; ser —   *to be pleasant*
agradecer   *to thank*
agua (f)   *water*; — caliente *hot water*; — fría   *cold water*
ahí   *there*
ahora   *now*
al (a + el)   *to the*; — + *infinitive   on* + *gerund*
alegrarse   *to be glad*
alegre   *glad, happy*

algo   *something,   anything*; — de *some*; ¿ — más?   *anything else?*
alguien   *somebody, anybody*
alguno   *some, any*
alquilar   *to rent, to hire*
alrededor de   *around*
alto   *tall, high*
allí   *there*
amable   *kind*; ser —   *to be kind*
amarillo   *yellow*
americano   *American*
amigo (m) — a (f)   *friend*
andaluces (pl)   *Andalusian*
Andalucía   *Andalusia*
andaluz   *Andalusian*
animal (m)   *animal*
anoche   *last night*
anteayer   *the day before yesterday*
antes   *before*; — de + *inf.   before* + *gerund*
antiguo   *old*
año (m)   *year*; el — que viene   *next year*; el — pasado   *last year*; este —   *this year*
aparcamiento (m)   *parking*
apartamento (m)   *apartment*
apellido (m)   *surname*
aprender   *to learn*
aprobar   *to pass (an exam)*
aquel (m)   *that*
aquella (f)   *that*
aquí   *here*
argentino   *Argentinian*
armario (m)   *wardrobe, cupboard*
arriba   *upstairs*
artista (mf)   *artist*
ascensor (m)   *lift*

asiento (m)   *seat*
aún   *still, yet*
australiano   *Australian*
autobús (m)   *bus*
autopista (f)   *motorway*
avenida (f)   *avenue*
avión (m)   *aeroplane*
ayer   *yesterday*
ayudar   *to help*
ayuntamiento (m)   *town-hall*
azúcar (m)   *sugar*
azul   *blue*

bailar   *to dance*
bajar   *to go down, to bring down*
bajarse   *to get off*
bajo   *short*
balcón (m)   *balcony*
banco (m)   *bank*
bañarse   *to bathe, to have a bath*
baño (m)   *bath, bathroom*
bar (m)   *bar*
barato   *cheap*
barco (m)   *boat, ship*
bastante   *quite*
beber   *to drink*
bien   *well, good*; sentirse —   *to feel well*
billete (m)   *ticket*
blanco   *white*
blusa (f)   *blouse*
bocadillo (m)   *sandwich*
bolsa (f)   *bag*
bolso (m)   *handbag*
bonito   *nice, pretty*
botella (f)   *bottle*
brasileño   *Brazilian*
británico   *British*
buenas noches   *good evening/night*
buenas tardes   *good afternoon*
bueno   *good*
buenos días   *good morning*
buen tiempo   *good weather*
buscar   *to look for, to fetch*

cabeza (f)   *head*
caer   *to fall*
café (m)   *coffee, coffee shop*
cafetería (f)   *snack bar, coffee shop*
caja (f)   *box*
calcetines (mpl)   *socks*
caliente   *hot*
calor (m)   *heat*; hace —   *it is hot*
caluroso (adj)   *hot*
calle (f)   *street*
cama (f)   *bed*
cámara (f)   *camera*
camarero (m)   *waiter*
cambiar   *to change*
cambio (m)   *change*
camisa (f)   *shirt*
camping (m)   *camping*
campo (m)   *countryside*
canadiense   *Canadian*
cansado   *tired*; estar —   *to be tired*
capaz   *able, capable*; ser —   *to be able*
capital (f)   *capital*
carácter (m)   *character*
carne (f)   *meat*; — de vaca   *beef*
carnicería (f)   *butcher's*
caro   *expensive*
carretera (f)   *main road, highway*
carta (f)   *letter*
cartera (f)   *briefcase*
casa (f)   *house, home*
casado   *married*
casarse   *to get married*
casi   *almost*
caso (m)   *case*; en ese —   *in that case*; hacerle — a alguien   *to pay attention to somebody*
castellano   *Castilian (Spanish)*
castillo (m)   *castle*
Cataluña   *Catalonia*
catedral (f)   *cathedral*
ceder   *to give way*; ceda el paso   *give way (traffic)*
cena (f)   *dinner*

cenar   *to have dinner*
cepillo (m)   *brush*; — de   dientes   *tooth brush*
cerca   *near*
cerilla (f)   *match*
cero   *zero*
cerrado   *closed, shut*
cerrar   *to close, to shut*
cerveza (f)   *beer*
cierto   *true*
cigarrillo (m)   *cigarette*
cine (m)   *cinema*
cinta (f)   *tape*
cita (f)   *appointment*; tener una —
   to have an appointment
ciudad (f)   *city, town*
claro   *certainly*
clase (f)   *class, lesson*
clima (m)   *climate*
club (m)   *club*
cocina (f)   *kitchen*
coche (m)   *car*
coger   *to catch*
colegio (m)   *school*
color (m)   *colour*; — naranja *orange*
comenzar   *to begin, to start*; —
   a   *to begin to*
comer   *to eat*
comida (f)   *lunch, food*
¿cómo?   *how?*; *pardon me?* ¿—
   es?   *what is it like?* ¿—está
   Vd.?   *how are you?* ¿—estás?
   (fam.)   *how are you?* ¿—se
   dice?   *how do you say it?* ¿—se
   escribe?   *how do you spell it?* ¿—
   se llama Vd.?   *what's your name?*
   ¿—te   llamas?   (fam.)   *what's
   your   name?* ¿—se   pronuncia?   *how   do   you   pronounce
   it?*
cómo no   *certainly*
compañia   (f)   *company*; — Telefónica *Telephone Company*
comprar   *to buy*
comprender   *to understand*

comprobar   *to check*
con   *with*
conducir   *to drive*
confortable   *comfortable*
conmigo   *with me*
conocer   *to know, to meet*
conseguir   *to get*
considerar   *to consider*
consulado (m)   *consulate*
contar   *to tell, to say*
contestar   *to answer*
contigo (fam.)   *with you*
continuar   *to continue*
convencido: estar — *to be convinced*
corregir   *to correct*
Correos: oficina de — *post-office*
correr   *to run*
correspondencia (f)   *mail*
cortarse   *to cut oneself*
costa (f)   *coast*
creer   *to think, to believe*
cruzar   *to cross*
cuadro (m)   *picture, painting*
¿cuál?   *which?,   what?* ¿—es?
   (pl)   *which, what?*
cual: el, la — *which, that*
¿cuándo?   *when?*
¿cuánto?   *how much?* ¿ – s? *how
   many?* ¿—años tiene Vd.? *how
   old are you?* ¿—años tienes?
   (fam.)   *how old are you?*
cuarto   (m)   *quarter;   room;*
   (ordinal)   *fourth*; — de   hora
   quarter   of   an   hour; — de
   baño *bathroom*
cuchara (f)   *spoon*
cuenta (f)   *bill*
cuero (m)   *leather*
cuidado (m)   *care*; tener — *to be
   careful*
curso (m)   *course*
cuyo   *whose*
chaqueta (f)   *jacket*
cheque (m)   *cheque*; — de   viajero

traveller's cheque
chico (m) *boy*
chileno *Chilean*

dar *to give;* —a *to face;* —
igual *to be all the same;* —lo
mismo *to be all the same;* —un
paseo *to go for a walk;* —una
vuelta *to go for a walk;*
de *of, from, by, in, about;* ¿—
dónde es Vd.? *where are you from?*
¿—dónde eres?* (fam) *where are
you from?* ¿—qué color es? *what
colour is it?* ¿—quién es? *whose
is it?* ser— *to be from*
debajo de *underneath*
deber *must, ought to*
décimo *tenth*
decir *to say*
declarar *to declare*
dejar *to leave, to let;* —de *to stop,
to give up*
del (de+el) *of the*
delante (de) *in front (of)*
delgado *thin*
demasiado *too, too much*
dentista (mf) *dentist*
dentro (de) *inside, within*
deporte(s) (m) *sport*
derecha (f) *right;* a la— *on the
right*
desayunar *to have breakfast*
desayuno (m) *breakfast*
descansar *to rest*
desde *from;* —luego *certainly*
desear *to wish, to want;* ¿qué
desea? *can I help you?*
despertar(se) *to wake up*
después *afterwards;* —de *after*
detrás (de) *behind*
devolver *to return (something)*
día (m) *day*
diario (m) *newspaper, daily*
diciembre *December*
diferente *different*

dificil *difficult*
dificultad (f) *difficulty*
¿dígame? *hello? (telephone), can I
help you?*
dinero (m) *money*
disco (m) *record*
dispuesto: estar— *to be willing*
doblar *to turn*
doctor/a *doctor*
documento (m) *document*
dólar (m) *dollar*
doler *to hurt, to ache*
dolor (m) *pain*
domingo *Sunday*
donde *where*
¿dónde? *where?* ¿de—? *from
where?*
dormir *to sleep;* —se *to fall
asleep*
dormitorio (m) *bedroom*
ducha (f) *shower*
durante *during*
durar *to last*

e *and (before* i)
echar una carta *to post a letter*
ejemplo (m) *example*
el (m) *the;* — cual *which, that;*
—que *which, that;* —más *the
most;* —(lunes) *on (Monday)*
él *he, him*
elegir *to choose*
ella *she, her*
ellos *they, them*
empezar *to begin, start*
en *in, on, at, by, about*
encantado *pleased to meet you;
delighted*
encender *to turn on, to light*
encima (de) *over, on top*
encontrar *to find*
enero *January*
enfermo *ill*
enfrente (de) *opposite*
enseñar *to teach*

entender   *to understand*
entonces   *then*
entrada (f)   *ticket*
entrar   *to go in*
entre   *between*
enviar   *to send*
envolver   *to wrap*
equipaje (m)   *luggage*
equivocarse   *to make a mistake*
escocés   *Scottish*
escoger   *to choose*
escribir   *to write*
escrito: estar —   *to be written*
escuchar   *to listen to;* — la radio
    to listen to the radio
escuela (f)   *school*
ese (m)   *that (adj.)*
ése (m)   *that (pron.)*
eso   *that (neuter);* — es   *that's it;*
    por —   *that's why*
España   *Spain*
español   *Spanish*
especial   *special*
esperar   *to wait, to hope*
esquina (f)   *corner*
estación (f)   *station;* — de auto-
    buses   *bus-station;* — de servicio
    service-station
estadio (m)   *stadium*
estar   *to be;* — acostado   *to be in
    bed;* — bien   *to be well;* — con-
    tento   *to   be   happy;* — con-
    vencido   *to be convinced;* — de
    acuerdo   *to   agree;* — dispuesto
    to be willing; — escrito   *to be
    written;* — mal   *to   be   unwell;*
    — muerto   *to   be   dead;* — pre-
    ocupado   *to   be   worried;* —
    seguro   *to be sure;* — sentado
    to be sitting
este (m)   *east*
este (m)   *this (adj)*
éste (m)   *this (pron)*
esto   *this (neuter)*
estómago (m)   *stomach*

estrella (f)   *star*
estropeado   *damaged, out of order*
estropearse   *to   break,   to   get
    damaged*
estudiante (mf)   *student*
estudiar   *to study*
estupendo   *wonderful, fantastic*
examen (m)   *exam*
excelente   *excellent*
excursión (f)   *excursion*
éxito (m)   *success*
explicar   *to explain*
extranjero/a   *foreigner;* al— *ab-
    road;* en el— *abroad*
extraño   *strange*

fábrica (f)   *factory*
fácil   *easy*
falda (f)   *skirt*
falta: hacer— *to be necessary*
familia (f)   *family*
fantástico   *fantastic*
farmacia (f)   *chemist's*
favor: hacer el— de   *please;* por —
    please
febrero   *February*
fecha (f)   *date*
feliz   *happy*
fiebre (f)   *fever, temperature*
fiesta (f)   *party*
fin (m)   *end;* por — *at last;* — de
    semana   *weekend*
final (m)   *end*
firmar   *to sign*
flor (f)   *flower*
foto (f)   *photo*
fracasar   *to fail*
francés   *French*
fresco   *cool, fresh*
frío   *cold*
fruta (f)   *fruit*
fuego (m)   *light, fire*
fuera (de)   *outside*
fumar   *to smoke*

funcionar   *to work (machine)*
fútbol (m)   *football*

gafas (fpl)   *glasses*
galés   *Welsh*
ganar   *to earn, to win*
garaje (m)   *garage*
gasolina (f)   *petrol*; —normal *two-star*; —super *four-star*
general: por lo—   *generally*
generalmente   *generally*
gente (f)   *people*
gordo   *fat*
gracias   *thank you*; muchas—
   thank you very much;
   muchísimas—   *many thanks*
grado (m)   *degree*
grande   *big, large*
gris   *grey*
guía (mf)   *guide*
gustar   *to like*; me gusta   *I like it*;
   ¿le gusta? *do you like it?* ¿te
   gusta? (fam) *do you like it?*

haber   (auxiliary)   *to have*; —
   terminado   *to have finished*
habitación (f)   *room, bedroom*; —
   doble   *double room*; —individual   *single room*
hablar   *to speak*; —por teléfono *to
   telephone*
hace buen tiempo   *the weather is
   good*; —calor   *it is hot*; —
   fresco   *it is cool*; —frío   *it is
   cold*; —mal tiempo   *the weather
   is bad*; —sol   *it is sunny*; —
   viento   *it is windy*
hacer   *to do, to make*; hace x
   días   *for x days, x days ago*; hace
   x tiempo   *for x time, x time
   ago*; — el favor de   *please*; —
   falta   *to be necessary*; —le caso a
   alguien   *to pay attention to
   somebody*; —una   pregunta   *to
   ask a question*
hacia   *towards*

hallar(se)   *to find (oneself), to be
   situated*
hambre (m)   *hunger*; tener—   *to
   be hungry*
hasta   *until*; —luego   *see you
   later, goodbye*; —mañana   *till
   tomorrow*
hay   *there is, there are*; —que   *one
   has to*
herirse   *to hurt oneself*
hermana (f)   *sister*
hermano (m)   *brother*
hija (f)   *daughter*
hijo (m)   *son*
hola   *hello*
hombre (m)   *man*
¡hombre!   *really?*
hora (f)   *hour*; ¿qué—es?   *what
   time is it?* ¿tienes—?   *have you
   got the time?*
hospital (m)   *hospital*
hotel (m)   *hotel*

idea (f)   *idea*
idioma (m)   *language*
iglesia (f)   *church*
igual   *(the) same*
impermeable (m)   *raincoat*
importancia (f)   *importance*
importante   *important*
importar   *to mind, matter*
imposible   *impossible*
Inglaterra   *England*
inglés   *English*
instituto (m)   *secondary school*
interesante   *interesting*
interesar   *to interest*
invierno (m)   *winter*
invitación (f)   *invitation*
invitado/a   *guest*
invitar   *to invite*
ir   *to go*; —a   *to go and*; —de
   paseo   *to go for a walk*; —en
   (coche)   *to go by (car)*
irlandés   *Irish*
isla (f)   *island*

Islas Baleares   *Balearic Islands*

izquierda (f)   *left*; a la—   *on the left*

jardín (m)   *garden*

jefe/a   *boss*

joven (*young* (m/f)   *young man/woman*

jueves   *Thursday*

jugar   *to play*;—al (tenis)   *to play (tennis)*

jugo (m)   *juice*

julio   *July*

junio   *June*

junto a   *next to*

kilo (m)   *kilo*

kilómetro (m)   *km*

lado (m)   *side*; al—   *next door*; al—de   *next to*

lápiz (m)   *pencil*

lástima (f)   *pity*; ¡qué—!   *what a pity!*

lavabo (m)   *toilet*

lavar   *to wash*;—se   *to wash oneself*

le   *(to) you, (to) him, to her*

leche (f)   *milk*

lechuga (f)   *lettuce*

leer   *to read*

legumbres (fpl)   *vegetables*

lejos   *far*;—de   *far from*

lento   *slow*

levantarse   *to get up*

libra (f)   *pound sterling*

libre   *free*

libro (m)   *book*

limpiar   *to clean*

línea (f)   *line*

lingüística (f)   *linguistics*

listo   *ready*; estar—   *to be ready*

lo   *it, you, him*;—mismo   *the same*; por—general   *usually*

Londres   *London*

luego   *then, later*; hasta—   *see you later, goodbye*

lugar (m)   *place*

lunes   *Monday*

llamar   *to call*;—por teléfono   *to telephone*;—a la puerta   *to knock at the door*;—se   *to be called*; ¿cómo se llama Vd.?   *what's your name?* ¿cómo te llamas? (fam.)   *what's your name?* me llamo . . .   *my name is . . .*

llave (f)   *key*

llegar   *to arrive*;—a   *to arrive in, at*;—de   *to arrive from*;—a   *to succeed*

llenar   *to fill*

lleno   *full*

llevar   *to   take,   carry;*—(tiempo)+gerund   *to have been doing something for x time;*—ropa   *to wear clothes;*—se   *to get on;*—se bien/mal   *to get on well/badly*

llover   *to rain*

lluvia (f)   *rain*

madera (f)   *wood*

madre (f)   *mother*

mal   *bad,   badly;*—tiempo   *bad weather*; sentirse—   *to feel unwell*

maleta (f)   *suitcase*

maletín (m)   *briefcase*

malo   *bad*

mañana (f)   *morning; tomorrow*; esta—   *this morning*; hasta—   *till tomorrow*; por la—   *in the morning*; 10.00 de la—   *10.00 in the morning*

mano (f)   *hand*

mantequilla (f)   *butter*

manzana (f)   *apple*

mar (mf)   *sea*

marcharse   *to leave*

marido (m)   *husband*

marrón   *brown*

martes   *Tuesday*

marzo *March*

más *more, most, else;* —o menos *more or less*

mayo *May*

mayor *older, larger*

me *(to) me, myself;* —llamo . . . *my name is . . .*

medias (fpl) *stockings*

medicina (f) *medicine*

médico/a *doctor*

mejor *better*

menor *younger, smaller*

menos *less*

mercado (m) *market*

merendar *to have a snack*

mermelada (f) *jam*

mes (m) *month;* este— *this month;* el—pasado *last month;* el—que viene *next month;* el—próximo *next month;* por— *per month*

mesa (f) *table*

metro (m) *metre*

mexicano *Mexican*

mi *my*

mí *me*

mientras *while*

miércoles *Wednesday*

millón (m) *million*

mío *mine*

mirar *to look*

misa (f) *mass*

mismo *same;* lo— *the same*

moderno *modern*

molestar *to bother (someone)*

momento (m) *moment*

montaña (f) *mountain*

morir(se) *to die;* estar muerto *to be dead*

mostrar *to show*

moverse *to move*

muchacha (f) *girl*

muchacho (m) *boy*

muchas gracias *thank you very much*

muchísimas gracias *many thanks*

muchísimo *very much*

mucho *much, very;* —s *many*

mucho gusto *pleased to meet you*

muerto *dead;* estar— *to be dead*

mujer (f) *woman, wife*

museo (m) *museum*

música (f) *music*

muy *very;* —amable *very kind;* —bien *very well*

nacer *to be born*

nacional *national*

nada *nothing;* —más *nothing else*

nadar *to swim*

nadie *nobody, no one*

naranja (f) *orange*

Navidades (fpl) *Christmas*

necesario: ser— *to be necessary*

necesitar *to need*

negro *black*

neumático (m) *tyre*

nevar *to snow*

ni . . . ni *neither . . . nor*

ninguno *none (of them), (not) any*

niña (f) *girl*

niño (m) *child, boy*

no *no*

noche (f) *night;* esta— *tonight;* por la— *at night*

nombre (m) *name*

normal *normal;* —mente *normally*

norte (m) *north*

nos *(to) us, ourselves*

nosotros *we, us*

noveno *ninth*

novia (f) *girlfriend*

noviembre *November*

novio (m) *boyfriend*

nuestro *our, ours*

Nueva York *New York*

nuevo *new*

número (m) *number*

nunca *never*

o *or*

obtener *to obtain*

octavo *eighth*

octubre   *October*
ocurrir   *to occur, happen*
oeste (m)   *west*
oficina (f)   *office;* — de   Correos   *post-office*
oír   *to hear*
olvidarse de   *to forget*
os   *(to) you, yourselves*
oscuro   *dark*
otoño (m)   *autumn*
otro   *other, another;* —a vez   *again*

padre (m)   *father;* —s (mpl) *parents*
pagar   *to pay*
país (m)   *country*
palabra (f)   *word*
pan (m)   *bread*
panadería (f)   *baker's*
pantalones (mpl)   *trousers*
paquete (m)   *package, parcel*
para   *for, in order to, towards, to*
parar(se)   *to stop*
parecer   *to seem, to appear*
pared (f)   *wall*
parque (m)   *park*
parte (f)   *part;* ¿en qué —?   *in what part?* por otra —   *on the other hand;* por una —   *on the one hand*
partido (m)   *game, match*
pasado   *past;* —mañana   *the day after tomorrow*
pasaporte (m)   *passport*
pasar   *to spend (time), happen*
pasear   *to go for a walk*
paseo (m)   *walk, stroll;* dar un — *to go for a walk*
pastel (m)   *cake*
patata (f)   *potato*
pedir   *to ask*
peinarse   *to comb one's hair*
película (f)   *film*
pelo (m)   *hair*
pelota (f)   *ball*

pena (f)   *pity;* ¡qué —!   *what a pity!*
pensar   *to think*
pensión (f)   *boarding house*
peor   *worse*
pequeño   *small*
pera (f)   *pear*
perder   *to lose*
perdón(e)   *excuse me, I'm sorry*
perdonar   *to forgive*
perfectamente   *perfectly*
periódico (m)   *newspaper*
permitir   *to allow*
pero   *but*
persona (f)   *person*
pertenecer a   *to belong to*
pesado   *heavy*
pescado (m)   *fish (to eat)*
peseta (f)   *peseta*
pie (m)   *foot;* a— *on foot;* estar de— *to be standing*
pintar   *to paint*
piscina (f)   *swimming-pool*
piso (m)   *floor, flat*
plato (m)   *plate, dish*
playa (f)   *beach*
plaza (f)   *square*
poco   *little;* un— *a little;* —a— *little by little*
pocos   *few*
poder   *to be able to*
pollo (m)   *chicken*
poner   *to put;* —la mesa *to lay the table;* —se   *to become;* —se a *to begin, to start;* —se enfermo *to become ill;* —se la ropa *to put on clothes*
por   *for, by, because of, through, along in;* — aquí   *around here;* ¿—dónde?   *which way?* ¿—cuánto tiempo?   *for how long?* — eso   *that's why;* —la mañana *in the morning;* —la tarde *in the afternoon;* —la noche *at night;* —favor   *please;* —fin *at last;* —lo general   *usually;* —

mes/semana/año *per month/ week/year;* ¿—qué? *why?* — otra parte *on the other hand;* —una parte *on the one hand;* —lo tanto *therefore;* —último *finally*

rque *because*

rtugués *Portuguese*

sible *possible;* ser— *to be possible*

stal (f) *postcard*

acticar *to practise*

eferir *to prefer*

egunta (f) *question;* hacer una — *to ask a question*

eguntar *to ask (a question)*

eocupado: estar— *to be worried*

eparar *to prepare*

esentar *to introduce*

imavera (f) *spring*

imero *first*

imo/a *cousin*

incipal *main, principal*

obar *to try, to taste;* —se ropa *to try on clothes*

oblema (m) *problem*

ofesor/a *teacher*

ograma (m) *programme*

ohibir *to forbid;* se prohibe fumar *smoking not allowed*

onto *soon*

onunciar *to pronounce;* ¿cómo se pronuncia? *how do you pronounce it?*

oponer *to propose*

otestante *Protestánt*

óximo *next;* el año— *next year;* la semana—a *next week*

eblo (m) *town, village*

erta (f) *door*

es *well*

unto: en— *sharp; on the dot*

e *that, who, which, than;* la semana—viene *next week*

¿qué? *what?, which?;* ¡—(bueno)! *how (good)!* ¿—es? *what is it?* ¿—hay? *hello, how are things?* ¿—hora es? *what time is it?* — pena que *what a pity that;* ¿— tal? *hello, how are things?*

quedar *to remain;* —en algo *to agree to do something;* —se *to stay*

querer *to want, to love*

quien *who*

¿quién? *who?* ¿de—? *whose?* ¿—es? (pl) *who?*

quinto *fifth*

quizá *perhaps*

radio (f) *radio*

rápidamente *quickly*

rápido *fast*

razón (f) *reason;* tener— *to be right*

recado (m) *message;* dejar un— *to leave a message*

recepción (f) *reception*

recibir *to receive*

recordar *to remember*

recto *straight;* todo— *straight on*

región (f) *region*

regular *so so, not so good*

reina (f) *queen*

reir(se) *to laugh*

reloj (m) *watch*

reparar *to repair*

repetir *to repeat*

reservar *to reserve, book*

responder *to answer, to reply*

restaurante (m) *restaurant*

reunión (f) *meeting*

revisar *to check*

revista (f) *magazine*

río (m) *river*

rogar *to ask*

rojo *red*

romper   *to break*
ropa (f)   *clothes*

sábado   *Saturday*
saber   *to know*
sacar entradas   *to get, buy tickets*
sal (f)   *salt*
sala de estar (f)   *sitting-room*
salir   *to leave, to go out*
saludar   *to greet, to say hello*
se   *one (impersonal pron.)*; *oneself (reflexive)*
sed (f)   *thirst*; tener—   *to be thirsty*
seguida: en—   *immediately*
seguir   *to continue, to follow*
segundo   *second*
seguro (m)   *insurance*; estar—   *to be sure*
sello (m)   *stamp*
semáforo (m)   *traffic light*
semana (f)   *week*; esta—   *this week*; por—   *per week*
señor (m)   *gentleman*;   — + apellido   *Mr + surname*
señora (f)   *lady*;   — + apellido   *Mrs + surname*
señorita (f)   *young lady*;   — + apellido   *Miss + surname*
sentarse   *to sit*
sentado: estar—   *to be sitting*
sentir(s)   *to feel*;   —se bien/mal   *to feel well/unwell*; lo siento   *I'm sorry*
se(p)tiembre   *September*
séptimo   *seventh*
ser   *to be*;   —aficionado a   *to be fond of*;   —amable   *to be kind, polite*;   —agradable   *to be pleasant*;   —capaz/incapaz   *to be capable/incapable*;   —cierto   *to be true*;   —de   *to be from*;   —la(s) + hora   *to be + time*;   —muy amigos   *to be good friends*;   —necesario   *to be necessary*;   —

posible/imposible   *to be possible/impossible*; suficiente   *to be sufficient*
servicio (m)   *service*; —s   *toilets*
servir   *to serve*
sevillano   *from Seville*
sexto   *sixth*
si   *if*
sí   *yes*
siempre   *always*
significar   *to mean*
sillón (m)   *armchair*
simpático   *nice*
sin   *without*
sobre   *on, above, on top of*
sol (m)   *sun*; hace—   *it's sunny*
soler   *to be accustomed to*
solo   *alone*
sólo   *only*
soltero   *single*
sombrero (m)   *hat*
son   *you/they are*; —las dos   *it's two o'clock*; —las dos cuarto   *it's a quarter past two*; —las dos y media   *it's half past two*; —las tres menos cuarto   *it's a quarter to three*
sorprender   *to surprise*; me sorprende   *it surprises me*
soy   *I am*; —de   *I am from*
su   *your, his, her, their*
subir   *to go up*
Sudamérica   *South America*
suficiente   *sufficient*
super   *extra*
supermercado (m)   *supermarket*
suponer   *to suppose*
sur (m)   *south*
suyo   *your, his, hers, theirs*

también   *also*
tampoco   *neither*
tan   *so*
tan . . . como   *as . . . as*
tanto(s)   *so much, so many*

tanto: por lo— *therefore*
tanto como *as much as*; —s como *as many as*
tardar *to take time*
tarde (f) *afternoon*; es— *it's late*; buenas—s *good afternoon*; esta— *this afternoon*; por la— *in the afternoon*; las 3.00 de la— *3.00 in the afternoon*
tarjeta (f) *card, postcard*
te *(to) you (fam.)*
té (m) *tea*
teatro (m) *theatre*
telefonear *to telephone*
Telefónica: Compañía— *Telephone Company*
teléfono (m) *telephone*
telegrama (m) *telegram*
televisión (f) *television*
temperatura (f) *temperature*; ¿qué—hace? *what's the temperature?*
templado *temperate*
tener *to have*; —x años *to be years old*; —calor *to be hot*;— una cita *to have an appointment*;— cuidado *to be careful*; —dolor *to have a pain*; —éxito *to succeed*;— fiebre *to have a fever*;—frío *to be cold*; —fuego *to have a light*;— una habitación reservada *to have a room reserved*;— hambre *to be. hungry*;— hora *to have the time*;— miedo *to be afraid*; —que *to have to*;—razón *to be right*;— sed *to be thirsty*; —sueño *to be sleepy*
tenis (m) *tennis*
tercero *third*
terminado *finished*; haber—*to have finished*
terraza (f) *terrace*
ti *(to) you (fam)*

tía (f) *aunt*
tiempo (m) *time*; *weather*; a—*on time*; ¿cuánto—? *how long?* hace x—*for x time, x time ago*
tienda (f) *shop*
tinto *red (wine)*
tío (m) *uncle*
tocar *to play (an instrument)*
todavía *still*
todo *everything, all, whole*;— derecho *straight on*;—el día *the whole day*; —s los días *every day*; — seguido *straight on*
tomar *to take, to eat*
tomate (m) *tomato*
toro (m) *bull*; los—s *bullfight*
trabajar *to work*
trabajo (m) *work, job*
traer *to bring*
traje (m) *suit*
tranquilo *quiet*
tren (m) *train*
triste *sad*
tu *your (fam.)*
tú *you (fam.)*
tuyo *yours (fam.)*

ultimo *last;* por—*finally*
un, una *a, an*
universidad (f) *university*
unos *some*
usar *to use*
usted *you*
ustedes (pl) *you*

vaca (f) *cow*
vacaciones (fpl) *holidays*; de—*on holiday*
vaso (m) *glass*
Vd. (usted) *you*
Vds. (ustedes) (pl) *you*
vender *to sell*
venir *to come*; —a *to come and*; —de *to come from*; la semana

que viene   *next week*
ventana (f)   *window*
ver   *to see*; ir a —   *to go and see*; —
   la televisión   *to watch television*;
   —se   *to look*
verano (m)   *summer*
verdad (f)   *true*
¿verdad?   *isn't it?, don't you?, etc.*
verde   *green*
verduras (fpl)   *vegetables*
vergüenza (f)   *shame*
vestido (m)   *dress*
vez (f)   *time*; otra —   *again*; una —
   once; dos veces   *twice*; alguna —
   ever
viajar   *to travel*; —en autobús   *to
   travel by bus*
viejo   *old*
viento   (m)   *wind*; hace —   *it's
   windy*

viernes   *Friday*
vino (m)   *wine*
visado (m)   *visa*
visitar   *to visit*
vista (f)   *view*; — al mar   *sea view*
vivir   *to live*
volver   *to return, to come back*; — a
   + *inf.*   *to do something again*
vosotros   *you (fam.)*
vuelo (m)   *flight*
vuelta: dar una —   *to go for a walk*
vuestro   *your(s) (fam.)*

y   *and*
ya   *already*
yo   *I*

zapatos (mpl)   *shoes*
zumo (m)   *juice*

Grammatical Index